HOW TO
LIVE IN FREEDOM
BEING YOURSELF

HOW TO
LIVE IN FREEDOM
BEING YOURSELF

ANICETO MASFERRER

RESOURCE *Publications* • Eugene, Oregon

HOW TO LIVE IN FREEDOM BEING YOURSELF

Resource Publications
An Imprint of Wipf and Stock Publishers
199 W. 8th Ave., Suite 3
Eugene, OR 97401

www.wipfandstock.com

PAPERBACK ISBN: 979-8-3852-6219-9
HARDCOVER ISBN: 979-8-3852-6220-5
EBOOK ISBN: 979-8-3852-6221-2

VERSION NUMBER 121225

CONTENTS

PREFACE

HOW TO LIVE BEING yourself was the title of a series of three conferences that I gave in October and November 2021 at the Ateneo
Mercantil of Valencia. The aim was to synthesize the contents of
my book, *Manual de ética para la vida moderna* (EDAF, 2020).
However, when preparing the sessions, I realized that it was impossible to properly summarize it. I decided instead to focus on
a fundamental aspect of all human life: *How to live in freedom by
being yourself*, the title of this book.

To break down what it means to live in freedom into three
papers, it was necessary to address a fundamental theme, each one
related to the next, forming a coherent and complete whole, while
acknowledging that each part could be further developed.

In the first conference, with the title "What is given to me: the
acceptance of oneself", I tried to explain what is given to us. This
is everything we receive – this is everything that has not arisen
from effort and that we have received without having decided to
receive it. In this respect, Albert Camus said that the only relevant
philosophical question of the human being is suicide, because one
can decide whether one wants to commit suicide or not. About
life one does not decide, because we find ourselves living factually.
This is the first thing, but not the only thing. Faced with everything
that is given to us, we must ask ourselves what we should do: if
everything is given to us, in what way can we contribute to this
happiness? What should we each contribute?

This was the object of the second conference. Only based on knowledge and acceptance of what is given to me can I take the next step: the personal project. Hence the title: "What I want to become: personal project and human relations". It is impossible to have a successful life without a personal project. In my opinion, this project has a series of characteristics that should be considered slowly. Knowing and being clear about one's own personal project, being unique, singular and unrepeatable, is a necessary condition for living freely with meaning and perspective –no two lives are identical. Otherwise, one ends up settling for merely an elective type of freedom, rather than realizing a biographical project whose choices have coherence and meaning.

The third session dealt with the challenges that life poses when someone sets out to develop or unfold a meaningful life or personal project. The project would be of little purpose if the individual allowed the passage of time and certain difficulties to erode or blur it. Hence the title of the third conference: "Personal fulfillment over time".

In short, I began with the concept of 'what one is given' and the 'need to accept oneself', aware that this is very difficult for many people. Then, based on self-knowledge and self-acceptance, I discussed the importance of having a personal project, which is key to growth and maturity as a person. As well as this, I emphasized the place that others should occupy it in. And, finally, I offered some advice on how to carry out this project in time, which is the first gift, along with life, of which every human being is the recipient. There can be no human life without time.

Although the three sessions of this cycle were recorded and are available on the YouTube channel of the Ateneo Mercantil, several people contacted me to ask me where they could acquire the written text of these lectures, so they could read them at their leisure. Some told me that they had listened to them several times, or that they visualized them from time to time, relying on them as key points of reference in their lives. Others encouraged me to write these sessions down to facilitate their circulation and careful reading.

These requests have led me to publishing this brief book. I am very grateful to those who encouraged me to put the cycle of conferences in writing and to those who were generous enough to transcribe those talks and their subsequent discussions. On this basis, I revised the text, because while suitable for an oral presentation, there are some phrases that are not so suitable for a written text; just as listening to a lecture is different from reading a text.

In the revision I have added or developed some aspects to give the work greater coherence and logical consistency. This includes the first explanatory lines of the book and the introductory chapter on the postmodern myth of freedom, which helps to better understand the extent to which we can accept ourselves. The personal project and its realization in time allow us to overcome an erroneous conception of freedom which is unfortunately very widespread today. The fourth chapter includes another lecture, also given at the Ateneo Mercantil, directly related to the object of the cycle, but on this occasion with a more social focus ("Is an ethical civil society possible?"). The book concludes with an epilogue entitled "Living in freedom is a learned skill", in which I address the younger reader more directly. Perhaps the student who wishes to know how and where to start, as well as the teacher who wishes to improve his contribution to the process of growth and maturation—both human and intellectual and professional—of his students. To both I convey—with two different texts—that one is not born living in freedom and being a good teacher, but that one learns, and that this learning depends, above all, on oneself.

I would like to thank my friend Pedro López for reading the manuscript, which has been improved and enriched with his thoughtful contributions. I am also sincerely grateful to Grupo Editorial Fonte for the publication of this work.

I hope that reading this book will help readers to make the decision to live in freedom, carrying out a unique personal project that will fill his or her life and from which society as a whole can benefit.

INTRODUCTION

The Postmodern Myth of Freedom

THE FILM *CATWOMAN* (2004) shows how its protagonist, Patience Philips (Halle Berry), undergoes a radical transformation at a difficult moment in her life. This allows her to go from being a submissive woman always ready to please, to a woman "as sharp as a cat" with strength, agility and sensitivity in her senses. She is then capable of taking revenge on her enemies. "Freedom is power, freedom is power", she proudly affirms. She adds: "Freedom also of 'being able' to do evil". Indeed, if what is most important to freedom is the mere 'faculty' or 'power' to do whatever one wants, the logical conclusion is that freedom also includes the power to do evil. The one who does good is as free as the one who does evil, if that is what one wants. This is a Nietzschean conception of freedom ("will to power"). It is disturbing to say the least.

According to the postmodern myth of freedom, what one wants is good and what one does not want is bad. It is not proven that something that one really wants can be bad, nor that something that one does not really want can be good. It is a 'myth' because reality itself refutes such an approach. But when we come up against reality, sometimes it is a little late and it is difficult to change that paradigm of freedom. Moreover, one lives immersed in a culture whose teachings go in the direction of the myth, so it is not easy to realize its falsity and even less to speak out against it.

Technology and social networks are the perfect embodiment of this myth of freedom, and can become the main source of this concept of freedom for millions of people. It is not theoretical, but practical and daily. It shapes the mentality, behavior and moral personality of everyone. Indeed, social networks make it possible to live and enjoy the reality one desires in an easy, fast and agile way, filling the senses with joy—of course, beyond the possibilities of a cat. There, reality is not a problem: one can be anywhere at any time, even in several places at once. One can deify oneself, not only by enjoying the gift of ubiquity or overcoming the sense of limit, but also by being able to see, travel, shop, and talk with a simple click. You can show yourself to others as you wish, for example by hanging out with some and avoiding others. Online, it is easier to appear as someone you are not, or to mask what you are. Online, being cool is relatively easy. In the virtual environment one can cultivate and nurture their image, their appearance, their "alter ego". They can be the person they would like to be but are not.

Hence, social networks are a great showcase, full of pretty and well-dressed mannequins, like those placed in department stores. Lives without real faces that hide, deep down, an emptiness and a thirst for authenticity impossible to quench with the exercise of that freedom of 'being able' to do whatever you want. If others think it's okay, then I do not disappoint them, or fail them, or have them think I am ignorant or too smart. The fear of others' judgment or ridicule seems to be reduced, because the other is not present. When he is present, I probably am not. However, this great showcase prevents one from being oneself, from thinking for oneself, from expressing what one thinks, and from displaying a unique, original and attractive personal project for which one is willing to do anything. It is a real farce. A superficial life. A life without living. One does not know who he is, what he is like, or what he is for. And if he does know, he is ashamed of it, and may hate himself, in part or completely. If the past is added to this, those darker parts of one's own existence can become (almost) unbearable. We strive not to miss anything while being unable to appease the inner feeling of emptiness and of losing everything. This habitual restlessness, which sometimes turns into a kind of melancholic anguish, can lead to prolonged episodes of anxiety that are difficult to cope with. One feels the need for constant and hectic activity, to always be with someone and have something to watch or listen to. Standing still, being alone and silent seem to be unmistakable signs of falling into disgrace or premature death.

And what relation will standing, being alone and in silence, have with freedom? With almost everything. A 17th century German jurist and philosopher, Samuel von Pufendorf, said that morality is what distinguishes human freedom from animal behavior. And a contemporary French scientist, Blaise Pascal, pointed out that, in morality, the first thing is to think. Whoever wants to start afresh, to get out of this impasse and overcome this postmodern myth of freedom that leads inexorably to the hopeless impasse described here, must stop and think. This is the only way to discover that freedom demands living one's own life with intensity and fullness, being a protagonist, not an observer, and taking control of one's own life. How can one live in this way, exercising freedom in this way? There are three fundamental steps.

1º) Know and accept what is given to you: knowledge and acceptance of yourself. Know the reality, starting with yourself, and accept it: accept yourself as you are, with your lights and shadows. The first condition for a successful life is to accept yourself as you are. And for this, it is necessary to know oneself. I must know what has been given to me, what I have encountered, and from whom I have received the love I have enjoyed. This knowledge and acceptance provokes wonder and gratitude and anchors us in reality and protects us from the danger of living in ignorance, in lies or in appearance. Only from the truth of who you are can build a personal and genuine project, without having to beg for the respect and approval of others.

2º) Decide what you want to become: personal project and human relations. For the exercise of freedom to have a meaning that transcends a disjointed sum of banal choices, it requires a personal project that informs your whole life and that is not self-referential, that is, where others are at the center. Knowledge of reality and of yourself allows you to build, in a unique and original way, your own life. This is what you want to become, anchored in reality. This in turn brings fullness to what you are, your potential and what you feel called to. Personal project and human relationships are key, because they give meaning, depth and perspective to one's own life.

3°) Make this project a reality over time by exercising your freedom. To be fulfilled and grow as a person requires time. But it is not enough to let time pass. The use you make of it will depend largely on whether you become what you want to be, to bring your personal project to its fullness. To do this, you will have to overcome some erroneous conceptions of time, very present in this postmodern society (narcissism, hedonism and utilitarianism), which threaten to erode not only what you want to become, but even what was given to you and constituted your starting point. Here it is essential to exercise your freedom. With your freedom you will be able to make your personal project a reality and you will be able to unfold your personality, with all its richness and potential. Don't settle for less. *Don't try. Just do it! Make it real!*

Thus, it is not possible to live in freedom, and to unfold one's unique and unrepeatable potential, without accepting oneself, without having a good personal project and without being able to carry it out over time. Let us now look at each of these essential conditions.

Chapter 1

SELF-ACCEPTANCE

THE FIRST PRINCIPLE FOR a successful life is to think for oneself. "The first thing is to think." This phrase is not mine. Pascal already said it almost four centuries ago. Why is it that the first principle to procure a full and successful life is to think or to think for oneself?

Non-rational animals can have a full life if they let themselves be carried away by their instincts and enjoy a life sensitive to the world around them as much as possible. I enjoy thinking about birds: how beautiful it is to think about a bird flying with majesty, that they can decide at will whether it flies to one side or the other! Perhaps that is why I like the flight of an airplane more from the outside than from the inside. It is more beautiful to contemplate its flight from the outside. From the inside one can see what is outside the airplane, but not the flight of the airplane, its take-off and landing. Returning to the flight of the bird, this is not possible for the human being. I am not saying that it is possible for man to fly with his hands (indeed, this is not possible), but that a full life is not possible just by following one's instincts.

It is not that the human being must despise the sensitive life and the sensitive pleasures, which can also be good in their right measure, but it is insufficient. We need things to have a meaning. Animals do not ask themselves the question of things having a meaning or a purpose. Always following our instincts or our senses does not help us. It is difficult to discover the meaning of things without stopping to think. If one does not stop to think, it is difficult to know the meaning of things or even to confer meaning to things.

CONTEMPLATING REALITY, THINKING AND DIALOGUING

In order to lead a full, successful life, there are three intellectual activities that, in my opinion, are fundamental: **contemplating reality**, **thinking** and **dialoguing**. I believe that these are the great intellectual activities that radically distinguish us from non-rational animals.

The postmodern society in which we live has lost **the ability to contemplate reality**. As Hobbes said in *Leviathan*, "to know is to know what can be done with things." For Hobbes, what is relevant to knowledge is not the contemplation of reality, but the idea of utility, of what is useful or practical. What one can do or not do with it: how can I manipulate and transform reality? This is so because, according to the way of thinking which has become so widespread today, contemplating reality is boring and not very productive. Manipulating things is seen as something more attractive and stimulating. This way of conceiving reality and its knowledge is a problem and constitutes an obstacle when it comes to discovering the wonder of contemplating reality as it is and of seeing things as they are. Let me give an example.

I am sure that upon seeing the title of this chapter "Self-acceptance" many will have realized that this is an important topic because it is a subject that is never completely learned, even with the passage of time, and some will have said to themselves: 'Yes, I am interested in this topic, I am going to read it'. In some instances, this may have been the case. Other people, however, will perhaps read it not only because they are interested in the subject, but also because they know me, and because they know me, they see me with good eyes. These good eyes make people more open to hear and get a better grasp of what I am going to say now. The same happens with reality: if it is seen, or contemplated, with good eyes, with an open and respectful gaze rather than with a utilitarian and calculating one, it is easier to get to know it as it is, not as one would like it to be. Looking at a person or a reality with good eyes, in a way that is open, respectful, and positive, rather than doing it from the perspective of personal interest, is different. It completely changes the perspective. Reality matters. People can live with one's back turned to it, and the first sense that allows us to grasp it as it is—with its lights and shadows—is sight. Hence the importance of stimulating and acquiring the capacity for observation and contemplation.

The second major intellectual activity is critical thinking or reflection. Everyone is in favor of 'critical thinking', but few manage to exercise it on a regular basis. Some people even say that they do not think much because when they do, they get irritated. They may be right. However, it would be necessary to see what thinking means to them and how they do it. It is not possible to live in freedom without a minimum reflective capacity, just as it is not possible to enjoy a good car if you do not know how to drive it, or if you insist on driving it from the back seat. There are three interrelated premises that explain why critical thinking is the key to living in freedom: 1) an authentically human life is not possible if one renounces living in freedom; 2) one cannot live in freedom if one ignores the truth that underlies and reflects all that is good, beautiful and just, and 3) one cannot access the truth if one does not think for themself. Hence the need to stimulate critical thinking. The first area in which the exercise of freedom must be deployed does not consist in the mere possibility of choice, but in the capacity to think for oneself. Without this, the other dimensions of freedom are insufficient and meaningless.

It is more humane to be in error thinking for oneself than to be in truth having "assumed" it passively and uncritically. The former, if open-mindedness and a healthy critical spirit is maintained, will be able to reach the truth and experience its light and fullness. The latter, however, will never finish discovering its radiance, perhaps the same one that led Dostoyevsky to affirm that; "beauty will save the world". Freedom is as necessary as it is beautiful, but it loses its beauty if it unfolds on the margins of justice and if it violates the freedoms of others, especially those of the most vulnerable, of those who do not have a voice or are not strong enough to make themselves heard and respected. For this reason, it is necessary to stimulate critical thinking and encourage the expression of one's own ideas (because it is not possible to think well, in a complete way, without expressing what one thinks). Those who think for themselves can of course make mistakes ("*errare humanum est*"), but they would be even more mistaken if they did not think for themselves (for fear of being wrong or of looking bad), or if they were not capable of expressing themselves and having conversations with those who think differently. Thinking for oneself requires expressing one's thoughts and engaging in dialogue, and this expression and dialogue make it possible to increase critical thinking. This requires an attitude of open-mindedness, incompatible with prejudice and stubbornness.

One is born with reflective capacity, but not with the habit of reflecting. Critical thinking requires practice. Education should contribute to this, so the responsibility passes to those involved in teaching. To this end, it is essential to encourage a taste for reading, the intellectual curiosity that leads to asking questions and trying to answer them yourself first, as well as by using the Socratic method. When teaching a class, it is advisable to start by explaining the relevance and interest of what is going to be discussed to gain the students' interest from the beginning. You need to capture attention and interest in the subject matter first, and then pose intelligent questions that stimulate students' critical thinking.

This is the key: good books, good readings and good classes where the teacher questions the student, and the student tries to answer in a reasoned way. This is not easy, but it is the way that it should be done. Sometimes, it is necessary to require the students to engage in activities before they choose to do so themselves. Some time ago, a volunteer told me how she started volunteering at the Universitas Foundation: "I started volunteering because they made me". "Well, they made me at first, but after a while I realized that devoting time to others was good. I got a taste for it and then I chose to keep on doing it," she answered. This applies to the love of reading: we must promote some good readings in the hope that they will serve as a stimulus and contribute to the enjoyment of silence, thought and reflection. Those of us who read know that reading a book means entering the life and world of its author, who in turn has entered many other lives. One lives almost as many lives as they read books, which is very enriching. We must transmit this richness to students as soon as possible, with age-appropriate readings.

However, if the educational system does not encourage critical thinking and the expression of one's own ideas (as is currently the case in our society) it is possible to acquire it if educators themselves put in a little more effort. In fact, it is only ourselves who can learn; an educational system can facilitate it, but can never replace the need for each person to put effort in themselves. I usually tell students that my main mission in teaching, is not only transmitting the knowledge relevant to the subject taught, but also to help them to think critically. I tell them that I do not want them to think like me, but to think for themselves. They should ask themselves if that thought is really theirs, if what they think (or think they think) is something that they have concluded after critically analyzing it, or if it is something false. It may be something that is in the atmosphere, in the cultural environment, that they think is theirs when deep down it is not.

Following the philosopher John Finnis, I also often warn students of the existence of three obstacles that should be known and be overcome in order to make good decisions. Sometimes that decision about what is good, beautiful or true can be clouded by three difficulties: culture, self-interest and the strength—or virulence—of one's instincts or passions. Therefore, when we make a decision, we must think: "Do I really think like this? Or am I just following the majority opinion? When our own way of thinking is identified with the majority or culturally hegemonic way of thinking, it is worth asking ourselves seriously whether this way of thinking may be more alien than my own. In relation to personal interest or instincts, we should ask ourselves: "Do I think this way because I believe that this is the right thing to do, or have I reached this conclusion because I have a special interest in it, or because I feel a strong inclination that is perhaps blinding me or preventing me from analyzing it in a more objective way? This is not easy because there are inclinations and passions that can be very good and should be followed, but it is not good to follow all passions at any time. This judgment demands a rational or intellectual effort and brings us back to the first principle: to lead a human life that leads to growth and fulfillment as a person, the first thing to do is to think. If the education system does not promote the exercises needed for young people to think for themselves, to think critically, they can practice it on their own in their own lives.

At the same time, it is important to keep in mind that human beings are fragile and not infallible. As has been said, "to err is human". Therefore, it is not possible to possess the truth in a complete way, because to believe—or even to think—that one possesses the truth is a form of fundamentalism. In this regard, it is advisable to avoid two extremes: that of the fundamentalist who claims to possess the truth and that of the relativist who claims that everything is absolutely relative. The truth exists, so we must try to find it. However, we should acknowledge that it is not susceptible to being possessed in its entirety. Perhaps because, in reality, it is more accurate to recognize that the person who finds the truth is the one who seeks it with a humble and preserving attitude. This path to truth requires an attitude of open-mindedness and dialogue with everyone, especially with those who think differently to the way you do.

Hence the importance of **dialogue as the third proper human intellectual activity**. One might say to me, "Aren't there other intellectual activities besides contemplating reality, thinking and having conversations? As a university professor, don't you read or teach? Why don't you add here 'reading' or 'teaching' as other relevant intellectual activities?" For me, teaching and reading is dialogue; I cannot think of reading without dialogue. For me, to read a book is to converse with its author. For me, to teach a class is to converse with the whole group in general and with each student in particular. When I am lecturing and the audience is perfectly quiet, because by watching the faces, I am watching their reactions to the answers to my statements. Body language can be interpreted, which allows dialogue with the silent audience. As a teacher, I always learn from my students, not only when they intervene (which they do quite a lot) but also when they remain silent.

Reality itself is objective, but the perspectives we have of reality are sectorial or partial. We could say that reality is multidimensional as, it has many sides. Depending on the training we have received, we can be more sensitive to one aspect of reality. That is why it is so important to have dialogue with others. In this way one is enriched. One should be happy to hear an opinion different from their own, even though this is not easy, because doing so allows us to learn and develop.

It makes no sense to see discrepancy as an obstacle, as something annoying or impertinent. In fact, it is something positive and enriching in personal relationships, as well as essential and indispensable in any democratic society.

Those who think that in morality the first thing is to do (good) things, that the first thing is to act, are mistaken. It is wrong to maintain that morality consists in doing things, and doing good things. "Let us do good things." It is true that the first thing is to want to do good. Of course, no one would claim that the first thing is to do evil, for this does not seem to be the best thing to do. It is true that the first thing is to want to do good, but in order to do it, one must know how to do it, where the good is, where the beautiful is, and where the true is. The true, the good, and the beautiful are not always evident.

There are beautiful things that are true and good, but they are not immediately visible. And since they are not, one should never leave that research or inquiry to others, including institutions, or to the culture our lives are immersed in. They can help, but we should not adopt a model or follow a behavior by the simple argument of authority. It must be because we think in conscience that this is the good or just thing to do. Although this statement may seem a bit strong or radical, I want to make it clear: we should always do what we understand as good after thinking about it for ourselves. Hence the close relationship between morality and critical thinking. Morality is all about living a full life. Pascal was therefore right when he said that, in order to have a full life, "the first thing is to think".

LIVING IN REALITY: SELF-AWARENESS AND ACCEPTANCE OF WHAT IS GIVEN TO ME

Here, then, is the first principle: think for yourself and think critically. This is fundamental because happiness, a healthy moral life, and a successful life, must be anchored in something. That something is reality. That must be the fundamental reference. Reality is the great authority of reason and of moral life and, therefore, the key to a happy life. One cannot be happy in fantasy. One can be happy "only" in reality. Although reality is sometimes hard, arduous, and difficult to know, recognize, and accept, it is the only foundation on which a successful life can be built. A freedom exercised outside reality does not lead to human fulfillment, but to emptiness and dissatisfaction, passing through the tortuous and painful field of addictions and frustrations.

Therefore, the first thing in moral life is not what I must do, but what I have already done. It is necessary to start from what I am and what I have. We must acknowledge and accept it. It is wrong to think that, to be happy, the first thing is to do, to give, and to love. They seem like important words. In truth, they are relevant, but they are not always the most important. Above all, they are not the first thing or the fundamental basis of a successful life. The first thing is to recognize, to become aware that if I can do, give and love, it is because I have received before. In reality, the most important things have been given to me. Since what is most important has been given to me, feeling or believing ourselves to be self-sufficient is meaningless and implies that we have placed ourselves outside reality. We need and will always need each other. Recognizing and accepting the existence of a reality that precedes me and is given to me is not an invitation to passivity, nor to undervalue the importance of our own contribution and personal project. In fact, the knowledge and acceptance of what is given to me demands an active attitude to understand what exactly is given to each one of us: who am I, what am I like, what have I received, what have they done for me, what love have I received in life? In short, it is a matter of beginning with the well-known phrase found in the temple of Apollo in Delphi: "Know thyself". This is the first thing. Plato put this idea into Socrates' mouth when he affirmed that in order to govern others it is necessary to first learn to govern oneself, and that to govern oneself we must first know oneself. To know oneself requires an active and positive attitude, which demands using your heart, will, and reason. Only heart and will are insufficient in the search for our own lives and existence. Pascal said in the 17th century that "the heart has reasons that reason does not understand". When I refer to intelligence and reason, I am not referring to the human being's bare reason, but to the whole human being, including feelings and affections. In life, we make decisions. Sometimes great decisions can be made in moments of special lucidity and relatively quickly, with the help of the heart, and they last a lifetime. Sometimes the heart can be a good guide to know which way to turn. Reason alone would not dare to do it, but the heart gives the necessary push or courage to decide on something big and worthwhile, even if this is difficult. Reason is colder and more conservative. It prefers to wait and ponder things much more, and it may lack the boldness of the heart. The ideal is to try to find a balance between the coldness of reason and the passion or impulse of the heart, although it is not always easy.

Ortega y Gasset's statement is well known: "I am me and my circumstances, and if I do not save her, I do not save myself" (Meditations on Don Quixote, 1914). We might think that this 'need to know' and acceptance of oneself is an invitation to conformism or resignation: "What can we do, I am like this with my circumstances, there is nothing to be done". No, it does not go that way. This knowledge is important because it is the starting point. The phrase "me and my circumstances" does not mean that one's circumstances are always immovable, or that my response should be conformism. In the face of certain circumstances, certain means can be put in place to make them change: we must try to improve what is improvable. However, it would not make sense to yearn for a change which is not possible. We must distinguish between what can be changed and what cannot, putting effort into the former and accepting and leaving the latter as it is.

In any case, knowing ourselves is the best antidote against two great dangers: conformism and daydreaming. When we know ourselves, we can dream and pursue our dreams to try to make them come true. We should not cut off the wings that could allow us to fly high, nor should we give up the big dreams and aspirations that we may have. Those dreams and goals, backed by self-knowledge and healthy judgment, are a great stimulus for personal growth. My view, confirmed by my own experience and that of others, is that we can go much further than we think. To do so, one must break the ceiling of false modesty that is quite common, especially among young people. It is great to dream and to have goals. To work towards a goal allows the decision not to be a pure act of voluntarism, of the will, but an act that affects and involves the whole person, including the reason, the heart and the will. Therefore, self-knowledge and acceptance should not lead to resignation, but to astonishment, admiration and, above all, gratitude. This is a fundamental aspect in every successful life. A person who is not grateful, who does not have an inner disposition of deep gratitude for all that he has received in life, can hardly be happy. That exercise, that knowledge that leads to acceptance, amazement, and gratitude is what allows us to anchor ourselves and our lives to reality.

CONTRIBUTION OF OTHERS TO OUR OWN KNOWLEDGE

Self-knowledge is something that lasts a lifetime. There is no point where someone thinks that he knows himself perfectly. No, no one knows themselves perfectly; we get to know ourselves more and more, but we do not know ourselves perfectly. At the same time, it is necessary to contrast this 'supposed' knowledge with reality. I may believe something about myself, but then I must look at the impact that what I do or say has on my environment This is of great importance. We must have a minimum amount of sensitivity to the *feedback* we receive in order to confirm or deny our own supposed knowledge. This is a task that never ends, but it is not a solitary one. There would be many limits to having to know ourselves alone, since we cannot look at ourselves objectively. To know oneself, it is not enough to make the effort to get to know oneself. Instead, we must rely on the perspective of the people who know and love us. Hence the importance of our circle of family and friends. Having friends you really trust and knowing that they tell you things as they see them, even if they are wrong, is important. Having an external reference point who tells me what their perception of my life or my behavior is, is a great help. Having more friends and more conversations makes it easier to receive that feedback. Finding a friend with these characteristics is not easy, but when they are found they should be treasured. It is important to cultivate and take care of this friendship. What characterizes friendship is the ability to tell the friend the truth, who in turn receives it knowing that it has been told in their best interests, rather than to hurt or offend. "He who loves you will make you suffer," goes the saying. When you care about someone, you are willing to give them a hard time if it helps them to improve, and I think this is a clear sign of sincere affection or friendship. Therefore, this expression contains, within the framework of family and friendship, a great truth.

If in some cases, one finds that they have somewhat recurrent thoughts, or that it is particularly difficult for them to manage reality and the circumstances around him and they are producing a situation of distress or anxiety, perhaps it may be appropriate for them to seek the help of a professional. Sometimes the support of a professional may be useful. It should not be seen as something negative, but as a way of growing and maturing. If a person goes to many professionals for help for minor issues, it will be more convenient to turn to a good psychologist or psychiatrist if appropriate.

I do not want to be negative, but I see that young people today suffer more than young people one or two decades ago. I still see in students a great capacity and enthusiasm to live and realize their dreams. I am amazed to see them act: their eagerness to know, their curiosity, their diligence and their capacity to work. This is something I see every year and every day when I go to the faculty to work. I see, however, that many of them live under excessive pressure, even those who are responsible and who want to do something in life and who are more conscious of making the most of their time, of not letting opportunities pass them by. I see an inner trepidation, nervousness, insecurity and fears within them—too much fear. All this boils inside them, since they often have no one to talk to, and you can see them suffer. As I say, sometimes they may not have anyone to talk to, or they have talked to someone who cannot offer them the help they need. That burden or inner tension is something that you can sense without them telling you, although sometimes they tell you because they cannot take it anymore or because they are looking for a word of encouragement or comfort. You can see it in the way they act, the way they talk, and the way they relate to each other, even when they come to my office to ask me a question or to hand in work.

There are many reasons behind this, but I believe that this problem has become more acute in this world where everything is faster and changing. It is increasingly complicated and difficult to understand what is happening to society. The virtual world has escalated this trend. I notice in younger people, from eighteen onwards and throughout their twenties, that social networks have affected them negatively and they tend to suffer more. They can succeed, but they need to free themselves from all that prevents them from living in peace, without the fears that imprison them. It is impossible to live as if those tensions, pressures or wounds do not exist. They must be faced. The passage of time will not solve them; they will only become more severe, and they will undermine and wear us down much more. Pretending to live as if that part of reality does not exist does not change the truth. As time passes, the weights on our shoulders become heavier. However, this does not mean that we should not have projects and illusions. This is fundamental. Sometimes it is necessary to unload some of the weight we carry on our shoulders, as if it were a heavy backpack. We must let go of the dead weight that no longer serves any purpose At the same time, we must also acknowledge those weights which must stay with us.

ACCEPTING, FORGIVING AND LOVING ONESELF

In any case, I can only be happy if I accept reality, rather than run away from it. Therefore, we can only live with total freedom if we live within reality, rather than in a daydream. The first great difficulty is living peacefully and happily. The main obstacle that I have experienced at times in my personal life, and sometimes in the lives of others, is the lack of acceptance of myself. Not only do you have to know and accept yourself, but you also have to love and forgive yourself. This point is key. There are people who do not accept themselves because they are unable to forgive themselves. This prevents them from being at peace with themselves and greatly affects their relationship with others. Sometimes, people who are incapable of forgiving themselves have more difficulty in forgiving others, and end up treating others as harshly as they treat themselves.

The lack of self-acceptance is understood in the general sense of Ortega y Gasset "me and my circumstances": it is not me, but me and the people around me, the world in which I live, my neighborhood, my town, my country. This creates two obstacles which are difficult to handle: distrust and insecurity. And when these obstacles are introduced and nest in the heart, soul or spirit of someone, their reaction is to try to compensate for these feelings by seeking the respect and acceptance of others. Some people do not end up accepting themselves because they choose to subordinate their whole life to satisfying the expectations of others. In doing so, they renounce their ability to search for their own self. This is a serious mistake. We must respect others and help them as much as possible, but without stopping being ourselves.

Other people feel the desperate need to fill the lack of acceptance of themselves with that of others, going through life begging for the acceptance and esteem of other people, because they have not accepted themselves as they are. They need others to accept them, not as they really are, but as they appear to be. This is because they do not accept themselves, and they may even feel self-hatred. This is done at a very high cost. This cost is to stop being themselves, instead presenting a distorted image of the self and settling in that appearance; in short, they are settling to live outside reality. That is why, as has already been said, virtual reality has hooked millions of people.

How can we avoid this danger in our society where so many value posing and looking good? It is not a terrible thing to try to look good, but not at any cost, and even less so by losing ourselves. It is one thing to look good and quite another to live fundamentally for the sake of looking good. It is good to try to be pleasant or pleasing to others, but it is not good to live life on that basis, wanting to please everyone. Many politicians try to please everyone. I have never understood those politicians who claim that nobody will be disappointed with them. I do not know how they will do it, because this is not possible. How can this danger that is so present in society be avoided? One way of expressing it perhaps naive, but easily understandable¾ would be to stand in front of the mirror. I am going to say it in a more direct way: stand before the mirror, look at yourself, recognize and accept who you are, with your lights and shadows, and start building from there.

Every person's life has shadows: difficulties, weaknesses, or bad experiences. Everything that may seem negative "I prefer not to think about it," helps us to be better only if it is recognized and accepted as it is. This is not an easy exercise at all, but it is absolutely necessary. Otherwise, we would spend our lives complaining about how things are, about who we are, and who we are pretending to be, anxious, and running away from ourselves. Running away from oneself is the opposite way to freedom and happiness. It is the worst thing we can do, as it is the thing that moves us further away from the fullness that every human being longs for.

Therefore, the first thing to be happy is not to ask myself who I want to become, what I want to do, who I am going to love in my life or how I am going to love them, although these are undoubtedly great questions. The first thing, in my opinion, is to ask who am I, how am I, who has done something for me, what has been given to me family, country, culture? Regarding love – before considering who we going to love and how to love them, we must remember and ask ourselves what love we have received and from whom we have received that love. It is important to accept the answers that arise from these questions: accept it and accept yourself, because even the things that can or seem to be negative can be a source of great growth. Crises, limitations, obstacles are usually a source of great growth if they are accepted and well managed and can take us to places we could never have imagined. We should both accept and be grateful for our limitations, shadows and weaknesses. This is realism.

THE IMPORTANCE OF GRATITUDE

It could be said that human happiness is comparable to the beauty of a painting whose background is based on gratitude. Being grateful implies and generates many good things and drives away many other negative tendencies. It protects us against two tendencies we must flee from and immunize ourselves against.

The first is to make the effort to be ourselves, no matter the difficulties, defects, or problems: "when I don't have that illness, or that difficulty or that problem, then I will try to know myself, accept myself and love myself as I am". This is a mistake. This is an unrealistic approach because you will never have such a situation. You must live in reality.

The second perverse tendency is that of longing to be what one is not, what one cannot be and what one cannot become. A personal example: I am a scholar. Quantum physics is completely beyond me, so I could never become a university professor of quantum physics. It is better for me to accept this and live peacefully, without longing for something that I cannot attain or whose attempt would produce excessive hardship and difficulty, which is incompatible with the peace that a full life requires. What is the point of longing for something that is beyond my reach? The reason for these desires usually lies in a lack of self-knowledge and self-acceptance. When one knows and accepts oneself, one does not crave to be what they are not and cannot be, nor do they crave to have what one does not have and cannot attain. In this circumstance, gratitude is usually the best sign that one is in reality. That one knows and accepts themself as they are, and that one has a good base to have a full life, living in freedom and without fear of being oneself.

THE DANGERS OF LIVING OUTSIDE REALITY

Reality is the most powerful vaccine against several viruses that haunt us throughout our lives. I will limit myself now to listing and briefly describing some of them:

- **Insensitivity to see what others do for us.** Sometimes we may think that others do little for us and that we do a lot for them. On some occasions this may be true, but we need to become more sensitive: we often find it very difficult to recognize what others do for us. Too easily we take for granted what others do for us and this prevents us from appreciating and thanking them as we should. We should be like the people who react very positively and with remarkable gratitude to any small gesture or service: "How wonderful that person did me that favor! Even if it was a small thing, it seems like a big thing to them.

- **Lack of kindness.** This is the danger of becoming insensitive and becoming generally dissatisfied with others' gestures of affection or service.

- **Two extreme tendencies: 1) to stop making decisions that would allow me to improve:** "I don't want to make those decisions because then I will realize my limitation and I will get frustrated; and since I don't want to get frustrated, I prefer not to consider anything and stay as I am"; **and 2) to aspire to projects that completely surpass us.**

- **Fears and insecurities.** There are multiple forms: the fear of making mistakes, the fear of failing, the fear of looking bad, and the fear of disappointing the people around us. Our lives can be imprisoned by these fears and insecurities.

- **To live pretending to "prove" who one is, instead of showing oneself as one is.** Only the person who simply shows themselves as they are lives in reality. The other confuses reality with his desires and the image he has formed of himself.

- **Longing for the big and the global, neglecting the small and the local, the close and the concrete.** Hence the danger of the Internet and social networks. They can be helpful for the acquisition of information or knowledge, but if a person gets too involved in the virtual world, they may come to think that their worth corresponds to the *likes* received for a comment or a photo just uploaded on a social network.

What have I received and continue to receive, and from whom have I received and continue to receive? Acknowledge it, accept yourself and always be grateful to everyone, even to those people who may have harmed you at some point in your life, because even these difficulties can help us to grow, to be better people.

RECOGNIZING OUR OWN STRENGTHS AND WEAKNESSES

As has been said, to know yourself, you must look in the mirror and try to recognize your strengths and weaknesses. What are strengths and what are weaknesses, and what is the best way to recognize them?

A weakness may be that aspect of your personal life in which you find it difficult to do what you believe you should do. You think you should do something good, but you are not able to do it, you find it very difficult to do and sometimes you end up not doing it, or vice versa. Not wanting to do something and ending up doing it, or the opposite, wanting to do it and not doing it, are signs of a person's own weakness. It is a weakness because it manifests a lack of authentic freedom. Wanting to do something because it is good and carrying it out reflects a notable degree of freedom or self-determination. Believing or thinking in conscience that something is good, and it would be the right thing to do (or not to do), and not being able to undertake it because of the effort it requires, demonstrates a lack of freedom that hinders personal growth and the path to fulfillment that every human being longs for.

In a university classroom, for example, everyone is different. Some people will find it easy to start studying at home after lunch, another will find it slightly difficult to start studying after lunch, and another will find it nearly impossible to begin studying. This does not mean that it is impossible to do what you need to do. You just have to be aware of this challenge to be able to face it in a different way than the other person who studies with ease. It is good to be aware of one's weaknesses, not to lose peace, but to manage them in the best way possible, and thus gain ground for real and effective freedom.

FACING THE REALITY OF WHAT COMES AS A GIVEN

It is not easy to accept reality or to know those 'viruses' in order to try to be happy within reality. To accept reality, the first thing to do is to know it. Knowledge is activated in three ways: contemplation, reflection, and dialogue. The main obstacle today is that we live in a very noisy society, one which is constantly moving and changing. In today's society, the only important thing is what is happening here and now, which makes it difficult to find oneself and to safeguard the conditions for contemplation, reflection, and dialogue.

In an interview with Alaska many years ago she was asked: "Hey, have you ever stopped to think?" And she answered: "Yes, the other day. At the beginning it was very difficult and at the end it was very boring. I made a decision never to do it again." I am sure you do not think like that nowadays, but this is what happens to many of us—it is hard for us to stop and think. It happens to me. I find it hard to prepare a text like this. I am a little embarrassed to explain how I prepared its fundamental structure. I knew before the summer that I needed to prepare this topic and I said to myself: "How and when could I prepare it? I would have to do it in August, because otherwise my day-to-day responsibilities from September onwards would take over. So, I took some sheets of paper and left them on a table as a reminder. I spent a month abroad on a research stay, and in the living room of my apartment I had those sheets with the titles of three parts, equivalent to the first three chapters. Days went by and I did not do it. Shortly before returning to Spain, I thought: "I have to prepare it because it is already a bit embarrassing that I have these pages here as a reminder and I have not done anything". One afternoon, before I left, I began and prepared a small part of the first chapter. Then I made the decision to finish it on my return flight. Why? Because there I was and I thought: "I have no escape here: I can't leave or go anywhere. I have to prepare this, with the page in front of me", and that is what I did. Why did it take so much for me to begin? Because its preparation required me to think; it was not a mechanical activity, but an intellectual effort, which is always a costly thing.

We all find it hard to stop and think. As you have read, I too find it hard to stop and think, even though I dedicate myself to thinking. It is easier for me to make a phone call or do a specific task than to write something or make an outline that requires intellectual effort. Stopping to think costs more and this is the main obstacle. This does not mean that when we manage to stop and think that we always get it right; sometimes we stop to think and we do not get it right. We can make mistakes. However, I am one of those who thinks that it is better to think and get it wrong than to get it right without thinking. Others think that it is preferable not to think so they do not make a mistake. However, this itself is the mistake: you cannot grow and improve without making mistakes.

Can acceptance of reality imply conforming to it? Indeed, reality can be very different depending on whether one was born in one place or another. There is no need to think of the Third World or developing countries. Even in the same city, people living in one street or another, or in the next neighborhood, can be quite different. Adapting to reality can hinder growth, but it is important to know this from the outset because this knowledge can be decisive and this is part of the content of the second chapter when deciding the type of personal project I want to create to change or improve this reality a little.

MAKING DECISIONS FOR YOURSELF

Is it possible to make decisions for yourself? There are moments in people's lives when someone can influence you very positively. When I was 16, I had a high school teacher who helped me a lot. Some conversations I had with him opened my mind. Some books he recommended helped me a lot. Reflecting and engaging with those people whose conversation stimulates thought can contribute enormously to a person's process of development. A point can come where he has learned to think and make decisions for himself.

It is true that there are people whose way of being can facilitate this process. But, far from falling into the determinism of thinking "I am like this, and I cannot change", what is decisive is personal attitude and determination. In my case, certain conversations and readings moved me, but the actual change depended on what I decided and what I was willing to do from that moment on. A conversation or a good text can help a lot, but the extent of the change depends on what you decide to do with your life. No one is born mature. If someone has a greater predisposition towards this maturity, it is helpful to recognize it and be grateful. But the rest of us, who were not born with this predisposition and have tried to mature through greater effort, and with the help of some readings or conversations, should also recognize it, accept it and feel grateful.

Giving a lecture on this question, I recall one person who shared a situation he had experienced, or rather suffered. The situation was about the influence of certain relatives or certain people who have power or responsibility over younger people. He asked me at what age I thought that a person is mature enough to be able to say that he is already himself. I answered: when he has managed to detach himself from the excessive influences of certain people around him. This is not an easy question to answer. It is not an easy question because a person may think he has managed to detach himself from the influence or his parents or relatives, without realizing that he has conformed to other ideas as a consequence of other influences. This is more likely if a person is "excessively sure" of his ideas and shows little tolerance for those who do not think as he does.

If you go to Kant, to his *Answer to the Question: What is Enlightenment?*, written in 1784, you can see how, in his opinion, maturity occurs when one is able to think for themselves. My impression of reality is that, in a noisy society, characterized by frantic activity, with so many people involved and investing so much time in social networks, people's maturity process is being delayed or slowed down. I have been at the university for twenty-five years and I continue to see the same yearning or positive background in all students. But at the same time, I observe a series of difficulties and situations that are different from those of one or two decades ago. The speed with which changes occur today makes a decade a long time and being only ten years old marks a much greater distance than in the past. This hinders the maturation process which consists of acquiring the ability and the habit of thinking for oneself to a large extent. Unfortunately, I cannot give a concrete age, since it will depend on what is given to each person, on his circumstances and, logically, on what he does on his part.

CHAPTER 2

WHAT I WANT TO BECOME
Personal Project and Human Relations

As WE HAVE SEEN, to be happy, we must anchor ourselves in reality. This is the most reiterated idea throughout the previous chapter. Self-knowledge is key to hold on to reality. This self-knowledge is the starting point to be able to accept ourselves – we must accept ourselves as we are, and recognize all that has been given to us, what we have received, and what others do and continue to do for us. In short, we must recognize the love that has been given to us. This leads us to gratitude, which is a feeling of something inner, heartfelt, and profound. Acceptance is the basis for other activities such as forgiving and loving oneself (and others). It is very difficult to forgive and love oneself if one does not accept oneself, with their lights and shadows. Therefore, without knowing, accepting, forgiving, and loving oneself, and being grateful, it is not possible to be happy.

Hence, the first thing to move towards a full or successful life is not to give and love, but to recognize value and be grateful for what others have done for me, what they have given me, and how they have loved me. Grateful acceptance anchors us in reality. It is only in reality that one can be happy; not in ignorance, appearance or falsehood, and much less in lies. Therefore, the recognition of reality, of what I am—"me and my circumstance", in the words of

Ortega y Gasset-, comes first. As has been said, it is important not to confuse the acceptance of reality with conformism.

WHAT WE CAN DO WITH WHAT WE HAVE BEEN GIVEN: HOW TO DECIDE WHAT TO DO WITH OUR LIVES

Once we accept reality, a lot of work can be done. And this is where the subject of the present chapter, a continuation of the first, properly begins. At this point, we should ask ourselves: What can I do with what I've been given? And to what extent can I grow beyond—or grow through—what I have received in my life? We can, and should, build a beautiful and useful home that allows for personal growth or development on the basis of the knowledge and grateful acceptance of what we have received. Hence the title of the chapter: "What I want to become: personal project and human relationships".

If we extend the metaphor of the building, we must remember that it is unique and unrepeatable—just as every person is unique and unrepeatable. No two people are ever identical. In this sense, the scope, originality, and shape of the building depend largely on the decisions we make. Therefore, although the focus here is completely different from that of the first chapter, it is important not to forget its content because it is still key. Trying to carry out our personal project when we have lost sight of the anchoring in reality (the importance of accepting what is given to us) would be like starting to build a building without having secured its foundations. In fact, when deciding what kind of building I want to build and what I am going to do with my life, self-knowledge is key and essential, because one cannot decide everything. We must always start from reality: from who and how we are, with our particular abilities, aptitudes, and attitudes. Hence the importance of knowing and examining ourselves, to know what can be done and what cannot be done (or should not be done). It is a matter of reflection, of pondering, and of personal judgment.

This is where one of the previously mentioned 'viruses' emerges—the kind that keeps us from making decisions out of fear of failure : "Since I don't know whether I will make the right decision, maybe it's better to not make any decision, in case it goes wrong and people around me say that I haven't been able to carry out what I wanted to. Maybe it's better not to have any ideas at all".

Regarding capabilities and attitudes, it is worth noting that they are usually bigger and better than we think. Indeed, when you have a good project, it is easier to bring out your best self. This is not just a catchy phrase from self-help books ("bring out the best version of yourself", "be yourself"); it is completely real. When we find a project in life worth striving for and begin to overcome difficulties, obstacles, setbacks, heartaches and pain, we realize that we have managed to break through the ceilings created by ourselves and our loved ones and overcome the supposed limitations of our own abilities and attitudes. Motivation, imagination, and dreams are key to personal growth. This is not, therefore, simply a catchy phrase: it is as true as life itself. A minimum capacity for observation of reality, of the people we have met over time, is more than enough to realize this truth.

Sometimes I tell my students a personal anecdote. I tell the story of what happened to me in one aspect of my personal project, in my professional vocation. When I finished my law degree and was thinking about what I could do for a living, I talked to some professors. I had several options, and the problem was that I liked too many things. I then met a person whose face and name I remember, yet I have never seen her again in my life, which shows the mark she left on me. While walking around she asked me what I wanted to do for a living, perhaps because I was about to start my last year of law school. I told her about several possibilities I was considering, and I remember she stopped and said to me: "You have told me several things you like, but really, what do you like the most, what do you love the most, what is your dream? I did not hesitate a moment to answer: "What I would love is to be a university professor, but I honestly believe that it is something that is beyond me, so I think it might be better to look for another more realistic option, and to have my feet touching solid ground". She corrected me with these words: "I think you are wrong. If that is what you want to do, if you feel that this is what attracts you most, you should take it seriously. Only when you have tried it, using all the effort you can, and it has not been possible, if that dream has not been able to come true, only then you can abandon that idea with peace of mind, and devote yourself to something else, without the thorn in your side that you wanted to do something and you lacked the guts, daring or courage to really try it". That advice helped me, and I believe I devoted myself to what I do because of it. I am deeply grateful to that person for those words and that guidance.

THE LIFE OR PERSONAL PROJECT

It is important to add the adjective "personal" to the noun "project," because it is a project that accompanies our whole lives. Just as we cannot cease to be people, the project also lasts a lifetime. Let us now see what this project consists of, and the extent to which it is or is not desirable. If so, let us see whether it is possible to carry it out, and under what conditions. That is the structure of this chapter.

The personal project is the purpose, destiny, or path that gives meaning to a person's life. The personal project does not consist of an ambitious goal in life, nor should it be confused with something that can be achieved over time (such as getting married, having children, or achieving a professional position), because, if this were the case, the person who had proposed it would either be left without a project upon achieving it, or would be left frustrated upon not being able to achieve it or after losing it (in the case of a marital breakup, for example). The personal project is not so much a goal but a purpose. It refers to the type of person one wants to become, to a vital purpose whose attractive force drives the subject in such a way that it makes him or her willing to make an effort and renounce other valuable but secondary things. It is something that, pulling strongly on ourself (sometimes in a more or less passionate way), provides continuity, coherence, and consistency to what we do at any given moment. There is no moment or task that is detached or disconnected from that project. *The personal project is, in short, that which I want to become*—hence the title of this chapter. It is what I want to make of myself. It is that which gives meaning to my life, my contribution to society and to the world, and that with which I identify with as if it were part of my DNA. It is that which is already part of me but at the same time is seen as a mission. In the words of the Spanish philosopher Xavier-Zubiri, "one does not have a mission, but is a mission", the mission of becoming what one feels called to be . The personal project is that which allows us and others to grow and improve as people. Without the personal project, our own lives would be substantially diminished or impoverished. We receive an inheritance (what is given) and freely carry out a project. The realization of that project does not just benefit us, but also others, our families, the city, the country, and the world. One receives an inheritance and leaves a legacy to future generations.

The mission we feel called to is precisely what gives meaning to life. If it turns out that what I can do, anyone can do, then what difference does it make if I decide to do one thing or another? The difference is that the person is not functional and interchangeable, but unique and unrepeatable, which allows me to do things in a place, at a time and in a way that no one else can do. This gives meaning to life itself, which is seen as a call to carry out a mission. This call or vocation does not just affect the professional (professional vocation), but all areas of the person (human vocation). It is what makes us feel like; "this is my thing", "here I find myself", and makes us feel attracted to it, just as one can say—half jokingly, half seriously—that he married that person because she chose him and knew how to get married.

This happens in other areas of life, such as in the person's professional life. Sometimes, it is the profession that binds a person: they have found that opportunity, those aptitudes, those contacts, even when they have not put all the means at his disposal. Something similar happens with friendship: you "find" friends, rather than seeking them out and choosing them. You can "make" friends with someone you already know, but a good friend is "found" without deserving it. Those who cultivate their capacity for contemplation and reflection come to understand that a lot of the time, they have not made the choice but instead they have realized that there is a great bond and attraction between themselves and that person, that with this person they can share their whole life, or that this other person will be a great friend.

It is worth asking ourselves: Do I have such a project or mission? As the type of project I have just described is quite radical, there is a danger of settling for less. Along these lines, perhaps we should begin with a more basic question: **Is it desirable to have such a radical project?** Would it not be better to be more flexible, changeable, or spontaneous, and more in tune with the changing circumstances of life and society? Flexibility, change, and spontaneity are not only compatible with the personal project but are sometimes even desirable or necessary. However, it is incompatible with the impulsive attitude of those who are incapable of deciding to make of their lives something worthwhile, something to die or "kill for"—as the title of a chapter of the *Manual of Ethics for Modern Life* says—something that is really worthwhile and for which I am willing to work, to get up in the morning with the illusion of carrying it out, even though I know that it is a lifelong task instead of something I can finish today.

I think it is desirable to have a project that enables us to live a meaningful and purposeful life, one which allows us to write our own autobiography. We must each build our own consistently, unique and unrepeatable, upon which we can build and stand in a world where everything seems to be changing, moving, or temporary. We definitely need a project that gives, in short, consistency to our existence and to our life. Therefore, yes, it is desirable.

If it is desirable, we can move on to the next question: **Is it possible to have a personal project to develop these characteristics?** Because not everything that is desirable is necessarily possible. In fact, some very desirable things are quite impossible. That is true. In my opinion, it is not only possible but necessary to pursue a full and successful life, and therefore to be happy. Being happy is more than just momentary feelings of jumping for joy. It is about living with meaning. This means: 1st) committing our lives to "something worthwhile", and 2nd) carrying out that commitment. These are the two conditions for the possibility of the personal project. I need something that is really worthwhile and something that I can carry out.

Another question could be raised, related to the two previous ones: **Is a life project possible for a person who does not know why they came into this world?** Knowing why I am here is indeed a difficult question to answer. It would not make sense, therefore, to let the fullness that a personal project can offer depend on the answer to that question. Knowing why I am here helps a great deal, but, as has been said, we must make the best decisions we can within our own circumstances. The experience of feeling loved and understood can also help – those who have experienced love may think that they are here because they have been loved and, in one way or another, all or many of us have had that experience. Some time ago, I asked the person I was speaking with about his parents. He replied that his father had abandoned him and that his mother, due to various difficulties, had been unable to act as a mother. There are situations so difficult that they prevent a person from experiencing the feeling of being loved—perhaps because he has not even known his parents. I understand that such a person may harbor a certain resentment that makes it difficult for him to forgive his parents, because he did not have an authentic experience of love on their part. But I told my friend that there is something he could recognize, which was that his parents had given him the most important thing they could give him, life, and that he could—and should—hold on to it. It is true that this does not completely answer the question of why I am here, but it does answer part of it: I am here because there have been two people who, in some way or another, loved each other. In any case, I think that the experience of love and goodness can help us to get a glimpse of the beauty of the moral commitment to do good and help others. Perhaps we could add, from a religious or Christian perspective, that we exist because we have been expressly loved and willed by God. God, who is Love, does not—and cannot – disappoint. The fact that one has not experienced being loved does not mean that they have not been called to life by a loving design. This may sound very theoretical, but it is so only for those who have not experienced or felt it in their own lives.

1ˢᵗ) "SOMETHING WORTHWHILE"

What can this "something worthwhile" be? In every human life there are three fundamental choices. The first—perhaps I should put it in last place—is to try to do evil. I believe that the starting point is that almost no one will make this choice. It is quite another thing, however, for someone to do evil thinking that he is doing good (at least for himself). We all have experience of this, including myself. The second is to try not to harm anyone. This is an important option and a fundamental principle, both of law ("*alterum non laedere*", "do no harm to another", as Roman law used to say)[1] , (not in the line below) and of medicine since its Hippocratic origins ("*primum non nocere*", "first do no harm"). Doing no harm to anyone is the second option. The third involves a further step: it consists in actively and positively seeking to do as much good as possible—the more, the better. I like to stress the adverb 'well' because the goal is not to overwhelm ourselves by trying to do good, but to do what we reasonably can, with peace and serenity Doing good properly is to love ourselves and others. He who does not love himself cannot love others. It is as wrong to love ourselves so much that we feel indifference towards others as it is to love others so much that we do not respect and care for ourselves. Healthy self-love improves self-esteem, as it leads to doing good and loving ourselves well. And love for others leads to actively seeking them to be happy. In short, what is worthwhile is to love oneself and to love others, which in practice translates into doing good and also

---

1. Digest, 1, 1, 10: "Iuris praeceptahaec sunt: honeste vivere, alterum non laedere, suumciuquetribuere." ("The precepts of law are: to live honestly, to harm no one, and to give to each his due").

seeking it for others. A project is worthwhile if it revolves around love. Otherwise, it may lack the necessary strength to overcome the difficulties of life.

Self-love can be a source of immense encouragement for a person, allowing them to do many things. Indeed, a person can go far with the strength of self-love, but the strength is greater if as well as self-love, we add love for others. Therefore, we must learn to love ourselves and do good, which is a way to grow personally. We must also actively, intelligently, and positively seek the good of others. What is worthwhile is to do good and to procure it for others.

Therefore, a personal project should pursue what is good according to a person's own mind (because no one is in complete possession of the truth, the good, or the beauty: these are discovered through practical action). It is necessary to seek our own projects as best we can. In any case, a personal project that does not include doing good, doing what one believes to be good, and doing as much good as one can for others, would be fundamentally lacking. The personal project implies a willingness to be open towards others. It is directly related to family, friends, colleagues, neighbors, citizens, and to every human being. It has to do with the ability to recognize others as a reflection of the self, rather than as an enemy. Other people are different and the space they take up in the world must be respected.

Human relationships are a key element in making a life project worthwhile. This is why they are explicitly mentioned ("human relationships") in the title of this chapter. The care of human relationships is key because others are, and should be, an essential part of our lives. In an individualistic society like ours, we might think that other people are a nuisance or a hindrance, and that they waste our time. Although someone may be unwelcome or annoying at a given moment, seeing others from that perspective suggests that there is a flaw in my personal project and my conception of life.

2nd) "THAT I CAN CARRY OUT"

In relation to the good that I can do, this is the key question: What can I do to do as much good as I can, to help and contribute to the development of others, my family, my country, and the world? What can I do – taking into account what I have, what I have received, what has been given to me—in a way that allows me to contribute something to society in a unique and unrepeatable way, because if I did not do it then nobody could?

We are all individuals. We are unique and unrepeatable, so we are the only ones who can act like we can. There is no room for copying or thinking that others can do better than me. No. My contribution is unique and unrepeatable. No one can emulate or plagiarize your project, nor can you pretend to be a copy of anyone else. Therefore, within my personal project, either I do it, or no one else will do it. Every human life is great and essential, even though at times it may seem to us that ours is very flat, dull, or irrelevant. We all think this way about our lives because the essentials of human life are simple: we get up in the morning, we do what we can, we work, and we talk to others. It may seem to us that our life is irrelevant, but that is false: it is invaluable and necessary. It is necessary, not only in your family, in your work, but in your country, in your society, and in the world. Your country and the world need you. This is a radical truth, not merely an encouraging phrase.

Having said this, let us return to the question: What can I do? It is up to each one of us to try to answer this decisive question, to discover what we can accomplish and what our personal project can be. In the first chapter I recommended standing in front of a mirror, stopping, thinking, and looking at how you are, who you are, accepting it, recognizing it and being grateful for it. Here my recommendation is this: stop and think for yourself—about your personality, your character, your experiences, your attitudes, your virtues, your skills, and, above all, what attracts you, what moves you, and what you would love. In short, think about what you would like to become.

Sometimes we have a negative view of urges and impulses, as if they were bad in themselves. It is true that the road to happiness does not lead to following all our impulses, but it is one thing not to follow them all, and quite another to think that they are bad in themselves. Some impulses can give us clues as to where our life can go, what we can help with, what we can be good at, and how we can contribute. That is where the personal project goes, and everyone must see it. In this regard, it can be useful to have recourse to the sources of knowledge: contemplation, reflection, and dialogue. My advice is: think about it, talk about it with people who know you and love you well and, after analyzing it, make a decision that will probably be the most important of your life.

COURAGE AND BOLDNESS TO MAKE A DECISION

To make such a decision requires a bit of courage and audacity. It requires courage because everything worthwhile requires effort, and making one's dreams come true is costly. Thinking about the effort and cost required can be overwhelming and dissuade those who would like to make their dreams come true. It requires fortitude and audacity because the achievement of a dream may depend on factors beyond our control as well as our own effort, which creates the risk that we may not succeed even if we have made all the effort we can. Therefore, both audacity and courage are required. It is necessary to be realistic. Courage and audacity are required to start a journey in a boat. Setting sail is already a sign of courage. But, as in any voyage, unpredicted difficulties may arise. We must at least manage the fear of uncertainty and the fear of failure, which requires courage. It is worth mentioning here Kant's well-known text, *What is Enlightenment*, where he states that the two major obstacles to achieving the necessary maturity to think for yourself are cowardice and laziness. Diligence, fortitude, and courage are needed to face them.

This decision will give meaning and consistency to your life, stability in times of change, and inner serenity in times of difficulty. It will allow you to be the same person, even when your circumstances change over time. It will allow you to write your own biography with a thread that will give it continuity and contribute to the development and improvement of others. Is this possible, especially with the passage of time? This is the big question of chapter 3, where we will see the connection between the personal project and time.

OVERCOMING THE FEAR OF BEING WRONG, FAILING, OR DISAPPOINTING OTHERS

Is it possible to design a project that is apparently personal, but is not deeply personal? Instead, it is imposed by society or the environment. This question is related to chapter 1. The starting point is reality, which is marked by who I am and how I am. When someone tries to emulate the lives of others or acts on the basis of what he thinks they want from him, he cannot come to the right decisions and he cannot arrive at his own port. This can happen when a person does not have the resources to find themselves, or when a person has succumbed to pressures from others telling them what to do. "How are you going to study Literature or Art History? You should study Economics because you need to earn more money". It is not uncommon to find students who are doing the career their family or social environment has told them to do, rather than the one they actually want. Normally, this is not good. However, we should recognize exceptions, such as a person who was forced to start volunteering but in doing so recognized the benefits of his services to those most in need.

Some time ago, while giving a lecture on this subject, someone asked me a question that seemed to be personal: "If you decide not to carry out your personal project, would you stop being faithful to yourself or your purpose? I replied, first of all, that there was no point in getting dramatic. Then I reminded him that there are two things to keep in mind. The first is the fact that a person has imagined a project but has not been able to carry it out for whatever reason does not condemn them to unhappiness. We must try to make the best decision in the circumstances. If he believes that something concrete would be the right thing to do but he lacks the strength to do it, or if he sees that it is beyond him, we should let him do what he can. I like to use the adverb "well", so that no one can think that it is necessary to go through life fighting tooth and nail, putting huge amounts of effort in or doing excessive violence to themselves. There is a tension between effort which is good, positive and helps us grow, and effort which goes beyond this and ends up causing us physical or emotional harm. This exercise of judgment is up to each one of us. The second is that we must not confuse the personal project with a specific profession, position or professional milestone, or with a particular initiative. These may be relevant parts of the project, but cannot be the entirety of it. We are worth much more than a profession, a position or an initiative. The personal project can include these areas, but at the same time transcends them. True friendship is similar – it does not depend on a person's successes or failures at any point in their life. Personal fulfillment cannot fundamentally depend on the achievement of certain objectives. The attainment of some objectives can be a part, but never the most important. We can be happy and humanly fulfilled, even if we have not been able to achieve some of the goals we have set for ourselves in life.

THE CORE OF EVERY PERSONAL PROJECT

What is the essential content of a personal project? Can you include some objectives, while at the same time transcending them and making them replaceable? It must contain something that has sufficient substance to constitute a life project that is open to others, and it must give meaning to everything we do. It should not be confused with an objective. If that something that should give meaning to all of life consists only of an achievement, then where would the meaning of life be if that achievement were not reached? Therefore, the attainment of a concrete objective cannot constitute the project of our life. If we think about it a little, we understand that the personal project has much to do with the dialogical dimension of the human being, which is an attitude of openness to others, passing through dialogue, donation, and service. A further step is to seek positively the good of others, and this means loving them. What does it mean to love? In reality, to love is to want the good of others. Even if we make mistakes in doing so, wanting to do good is a clear sign of loving. Therefore, a personal project consists of a life conceived and lived with an attitude of openness towards others, seeking their happiness. From there, if a person believes that they can make this project more concrete through the exercise of a certain profession, such as by dedicating themselves to a vocation they feel called to, they can do so. However, this level of concreteness should not be the focus of the project because its realization can be frustrated for reasons beyond a person's own control, such as if the person does not obtain the position they aspire to attain. This often happens, but the person should still continue with their project of openness and service to others. Although some milestones or fundamental objectives of the project may fail, the vital project should remain, perhaps with greater depth after an unexpected and painful experience.

In any case, we must anchor ourselves in reality. If in reality there are circumstances which make it impossible to fulfil a dream I have always had, I should be able to turn the page and move on instead of spending my life regretting that I have not been able to realize that dream. I should close that chapter and do, with peace, what I can realistically do. That is realism, not idealism. This connects with the backpack I spoke about earlier, which contains things that exist and may not be easy to get rid of. The backpack may contain some weights that can be unloaded and others that cannot. Moreover, it may contain some weights for some people but not others. Maybe one person will be able to unload something from his mental hard drive and another will not. The extent to which different people will be able to empty their backpacks is different. It will be important to look at each particular case.

FINAL SUMMARY

I conclude with a brief summary. In chapter 1 we saw how one does not decide whether to live or not to live, whether to receive lots or little, or whether to be loved a large amount or a small amount. This is all given to us and it is impossible for us to decide whether to receive it or not. The only thing we can do is to recognize this fact, accept it and be grateful. In this second chapter we have seen that I can, and must, decide on the basis of what is given to me, of what I am and how I am, why and how to live. I must give myself to others and love them, knowing that, in reality, this means bringing to fullness who I am: being true to myself, unique and unrepeatable. T. S. Eliot stated that "[I]n my beginning is my end". In reality, this project allows you to recognize yourself for what you are because, deep down, it will lead you to the fullness of what you really are. You may think that many important things are given to you, and that is true, but personal fulfillment through a unique and unrepeatable project is not given to us. It depends on each one of us. And it depends on the decision to bring to fullness what I already am or not, to be true to myself or not, and to be myself or not.

My advice at the end of this chapter is simple: take your time to think, seek counsel, decide, and set out on the path of your life project. And if you fear what time may bring, let me reassure you: for those who contemplate, reflect, and engage in dialogue with others who share the same longing for depth, time will always be an ally.

Chapter 3

SELF-REALIZATION OVER TIME

It would be of little use to accept myself and what has been given to me (chapter 1), and to be clear about what I want to become—my personal project and my human relationships (chapter 2)—if everything then remained static. In fact, the title itself, 'Self-Realization Over Time,' brings together two essential ideas: personal fulfillment can only unfold over time, and it requires time. It cannot be achieved quickly or instantaneously. There is no single moment in which everything 'clicks' and a person becomes fulfilled. Self-realization requires time and patience. Many things can be achieved quickly—but personal fulfillment is not one of them.

This chapter is divided into three main parts. The subject matter is so broad that I will limit myself to presenting a basic outline that could be developed further. The first part explains why time is key to personal fulfillment. In the second part I describe the various misconceptions about time that are present in our culture and that hinder personal fulfillment. In the third part I point out some aspects that I believe are essential for overcoming these current misconceptions about time.

1°) WHY IS TIME KEY TO PERSONAL FULFILLMENT?

It seems a truism to say that *time is absolutely necessary*. A life without time is no life because life requires time to be lived. It is true that we are born and die in time, but here I am referring precisely to the fact of its duration, that duration that goes from the moment we are born until we die and in which we have the opportunity to become what we want to be by carrying out our personal project.

At birth, we receive life. Following Ortega y Gasset – "I am I and my circumstance" – each one of us has our family circumstances, talents, experience, and diverse difficulties, but to that life and circumstances we add time. Time is precisely what allows us to reach fulfillment, to become what I feel called to be, and to be what I want to be. That is someone who, in some way, is already in me or is already potentially me. The person I want to become is in me because I feel this call to be that which is already embodied by me. It is within my reach, as we saw in the previous chapter: "What I want to become". Precisely because it is something that is already within my reach, it is important to start from what I am and from what is given to me. We cannot, however, stop there, or let ourselves fall into conformism.

However, *time is not only necessary, but also fundamentally valuable*, and this is something we experience over time. A young person finds it difficult to value time, but he gains greater awareness of its value as he grows older and decides that he would like to make up for lost time: "If only I had been more aware of the value of time before!" "Late I loved you," exclaimed Augustine of Hippo addressing God, after he found Christ after many years of existential searching for Him without knowing it. The expression "Late I loved you" is apt: "How late I discovered what I really wanted to become!".

Therefore, time is necessary and valuable. Moreover, it should be emphasized that *the most valuable time is the present time*. This is not an invitation to ignore the past or to stop caring about the future. The past and the future are secondary to the present because *only in the present can I live fully*. I cannot live to the full in the past nor in the future that has not yet arrived, I can only live in fullness in the present. I cannot love in the past, nor can I love in the future. I can only love in the present.

Only in the present can we realize ourselves in conformity with our own personal projects. In this sense, it is true to say that *happiness is not only at the end of the road, but is in the course of the journey, in the fact of walking towards the final destination.* Happiness is in the present. The person who waits to be happy or pretends to make his happiness dependent on obtaining something or on a change of circumstances, will at some point realize that happiness has to do with the present and the internal. It is not to do with external factors or circumstances. Hence the primacy of the present over the past and the future. In life *it is important to try to enjoy what you are doing and what you believe you have to do,* even though sometimes you may not reap the expected reward of what you are doing. In other words, fulfillment or joy is not fundamentally found in the achievement of a series of objectives aligned with our personal project, but in the present path towards that project. Carrying out that project goes beyond the specific objectives that we have set ourselves.

Although the present time is valuable for everyone, it acquires even greater value for those who embark on a personal project that illuminates, informs and gives meaning to their own existence. Whoever views his life as a "destiny towards" their personal project not only values the present time more, but manages to connect the present (in which one is) with the past (with what he has been and what he has done) and his future (with what he wants to become). It is not a matter, therefore, of focusing purely on a present that is detached and isolated from the past and the future, but focusing on a present that is perfectly crafted in each person, in what is given to him and what he wants to become. The person who has a personal project or a solid destiny sees time as duration and his life as an authentic autobiography with a single character, a beginning, a guiding thread, and a destiny. This autobiography becomes a reality in the course of time. Over the course of time situations change, which modify and enrich us, but do not make us lose everything we consider fundamental in life. If nothing is permanent and everything changes, then the autobiography loses its consistency because the direction has vanished—the guiding thread that gave the central character a defining profile. In that case, we would have autobiographies of different "characters" or different autobiographies, but not one with one character that develops over time.

2°) THE CONCEPTION OF TIME IN TODAY'S CULTURE

After explaining why time is so important to personal fulfillment, it is appropriate to describe the errors of today's culture in the conception of time. Again, this is a complex issue that I will limit myself to condensing so as not to overextend myself and abuse the reader's patience, while also trying not to fall into an oversimplification of reality.

I think that *the errors in the conception of time in self-realization are rooted in three ideas: hedonism, narcissism, and utilitarianism.* Therefore, the errors in the conception of time are due to a hedonistic, narcissistic, and utilitarian conception of time. Hedonism is shown in the tendency to seek immediate and constant gratification in all things, which is common in our culture. We want gratification and to be able to see the result. Narcissism manifests itself in the tendency to do everything from a self-referential perspective, where everything is for me. At the same time, I ignore and undervalue other people. Finally, utilitarianism leads to confusing personal fulfillment with the achievement of objectives, so that you feel as if you cannot be happy unless you fulfil an objective. Utilitarianism is the extreme opposite of the morality this book puts forward, where the object of morality is to do good out of love, regardless of the result. This is because utilitarianism is a results-based morality (hence its close ties to pragmatism and consequentialism), where goodness and love are reduced to near insignificance.

Our society praises productivity and results, which creates a complex and highly competitive environment. It creates and cultivates an environment which gives rise to anxiety and frustration. This hedonistic, narcissistic, and utilitarian conception of time leads to a meaningless life because the only thing that makes sense is immediate gratification. The only guiding thread is the search for disconnected, unrelated gratifications, and the only perspective is that of the isolated self, incapable of recognizing other people. The isolated self is only concerned with visible and tangible results. There is no depth or profundity; everything is superficial and visible. Today's culture has not understood the truth of those wise and accurate words of *The Little Prince*: "What is essential is invisible to the eye".

This explains why *time is, for many, a source of fears and insecurities*. This is because it is not under our control. It looms into the unknown, overwhelming us every day and presenting us with unforeseen challenges that we do not know if we can manage. Sometimes we would like time to stand still, but other times we would like it to go faster, or for something to never arrive or to arrive immediately. Some people see time as an enemy and live against the clock, going through life as if they were always running late. On the other hand, time seems to test our endurance, our stamina, and our consistency. It is true that most of these fears are inherent to the human condition. Human life is marked, whether we want it to be or not, by doubt, fear, and trial. However, it is also a consequence largely of the current cultural conception of time, which I will now describe very briefly.

The postmodern mentality and culture in which we live has been shaped by the digital world. It sees the world from the coordinates of immediacy, speed, change and noise. These references are present; they are our coordinates. The good is immediate and fast, whereas the permanent is seen as repetitive, tedious and boring. There is also a lot of background noise. According to the bible of postmodernity, far from affirming that man has been made "in the image and likeness of God", it teaches rather that he has been made "in the image and likeness of machines". Human beings have become fast – minutes and hours have become unbearable. Reducing the duration of time to a succession of instances, reducing time to the immediate, has been the transformation in thinking brought about by postmodernity. Everything must be done extremely fast, at great speed. Otherwise, it is boring, tiring, not at all gratifying and, therefore, it cannot be good.

For today's culture what is good, beautiful, and true is the immediate, the fast and the easily changeable. Hence the admiration that our society and culture have for geniuses and gifted people. This admiration is because a genius or a gifted person is not only capable of doing complex things quickly with little effort, but also of doing them well and obtaining the desired result (therefore, with the consequent gratification). Hence, these people are admired. As are *multitaskers*, who do several things at the same time, the more the better. Our imagination judges something that continues for a short period of time as slow, and as fast what is immediate and instantaneous, that which is just a click away. That is why the virtual world is so attractive, because everything is just a click away, and you can always satisfy your tastes, preferences and passions with speed and immediacy. The issue is that this immediacy not only leaves those who experience it unsatisfied, but it separates people from human reality and leaves them incapable of carrying out long term projects. This leaves them incapable of living an accomplished life according to their personal project, which benefits not only themselves but their friends, family, and society as a whole.

Today's culture admires and places on a pedestal the extraordinary over the ordinary, the spontaneous over the predictable. It understands that the extraordinary and spontaneous are liberating, while the ordinary or predictable is enslaving. This is a feral spontaneity, which is nothing more than an unconnected succession of moments without purpose or project. In short, the subject who displays this spontaneity lacks an authentic autobiography. This short-sighted and distorted conception of the course of time is not only incompatible with authentic human personal fulfillment but also generates many cracks and inconsistencies in people's lives. Let us look at some of them:

- A person would like to make something great of themselves, but then lives in the present with their back to that project and makes decisions contrary to that project.

- A person is impressed by the beauty of great buildings or cathedrals, but is not aware that this requires years or decades or work and instead would like to build a great cathedral quickly. He is impressed by the Sagrada Familia, is not aware that this temple has been under construction for many years and is not yet finished, like the life of every human being. He would like to make something great of his life, like the Sagrada Familia or the cathedral of Burgos, but he does not want to go through the process of building and developing, day by day and little by little.

- A person may wish to turn their life into a romance novel, yet their daily decisions and actions do not follow the storyline they imagine.

- A person has clever ideas and intentions but does not make the effort to make them a reality on a day-to-day basis. Of course, it is easier to be carried away by impulses or by the circumstances of the moment. This does not mean denying the importance of circumstances, nor the convenience of valuing them. However, they should not constantly change the personal project. Otherwise, there would not really be *one* project, but multiple, as many and as diverse as the circumstances themselves.

- We can live an unsatisfied life, because we have been bogged down by immediate gratifications, and we have become desensitized to ourselves and others. This happens because we have become depersonalized, and have become alien even to ourselves.

Time can erode everything. It can erode not only that personal project that fills our lives with meaning, but even the gift of human life that allows us to 1) live it with wonder and gratitude—as we saw in chapter 1—and 2) to recognize ourselves in others, whom we care for, listen to and learn from, with whom we grow as people.

3°) HOW TO OVERCOME THE DIFFICULTIES AND DANGERS POSED BY THE PASSAGE OF TIME

How can we overcome these difficulties and real, immediate dangers, so present in today's culture? Here are two basic ideas and nine key points, leaving the reader to think about them and develop them further and above all, to apply them to each case or situation.

Basic ideas

1) It has been seen that time is not only necessary, but also valuable. If projects become reality in time, the great project of our realization is only possible with the passing of time. This is different from merely letting time pass. The first basic idea is the following: *if we take advantage of (present) time, we can become what we want to be. If not, we can become depersonalized and dehumanized.* We have all heard the expressions "time will tell" and "time puts each person in their place". This is often, albeit not always, the case. Here we could develop the idea that time is a teacher. As Cicero said, history is "the teacher of life", and history is precisely the course of time. Time is a teacher (that teaches), a doctor (that heals) and a judge (that judges and does justice, generally putting each person in his or her rightful place).

2) Once you are clear about your personal project and you have decided what you want to become, my advice is the following: *make sure that time always plays in your favor.* This means that, whatever you do, you must make sure that your behavior always goes in the direction of your project, where you believe in conscience that your life should go. That will lead you towards what you want to become.

The fundamental question is how to make time work in our favor. Here are nine pieces of practical advice.

Practical advice

1) Try to think, act, and feel in tune with what you want to become. We would all like to write or make a great love novel out of our lives, but our daily decisions are not about love (as an aside, I strongly recommend dedicating some time a day to writing, because writing encourages reflection. You must listen to yourself. It should be a regular thing, daily if possible). We have good ideas and intentions, but we do not end up making them a reality daily, because we think "each day has its own challenges and we should not be rigid", but this takes us far from what we say we want as a project for our life. Gandi affirmed that "happiness is attained when what one thinks, what one says and what one does are in harmony". I would also add "what one feels", because the world of feelings and affections is as human as the world of intelligence and will. We must learn to ask ourselves: "Is what I am doing, saying, thinking or feeling in harmony with what I want to become? If it is, go ahead; if not, it is important to fix this, because this is not what I really want. And it would make no sense to change what I want to become passive to passing circumstances or desires. Obviously, we are not perfect, and we tend to deviate, but it is more harmful to fail to fix the course than the very fact of making a mistake or deviating itself.

The first level of struggle is that of thought. There are many times where we lose this struggle, and that is the first level where it is important to fight the battle to conquer our own freedom. A negative, vengeful, or envious thought does great harm to the person who admits it or does not reject it. We should nip them in the bud. Otherwise, they corrode us inside and prevent us from living in peace with ourselves and with others. Even if a person may have hurt you or tried to hurt you, you cannot allow any negative thoughts to arise against them, because you are what you think even when that thought is hidden from people and not translated into action. You are what you think, what you wish, and what you want. When you act, what you do makes you a better person or more miserable depending on what the result you want to achieve through that action, such as to help others or to hurt them. What you think makes you better or degrades you.

2) When you have strayed, recognize it, rectify it and move on. Do not get discouraged: *Do not give up!* Building takes time, destroying is amazingly fast. We all have experience of this. We destroy quickly and we build and rebuild with time. The less time you spend destroying by going in the opposite direction to what you had set out to do with your project, the better. We must always be building, even if it is step by step, slowly. We build little by little. The example of the temple of the Sagrada Familia or the cathedral of Burgos was mentioned earlier. He who works and lays bricks every day throughout his life ends up building something great and lasting, whereas he who changes his plan every day makes it far more difficult for himself to achieve something valuable. Even if he is a genius, his personal realization may suffer from his spontaneity. Indeed, we build slowly towards a clear direction and destination. Perhaps we would like to go faster, but we should not get impatient and instead keep moving in that direction little by little, even if it is at a snail's pace. If I am going in the right direction, time is on my side.

Whoever has a destiny or pursues a vital goal examines his conduct daily and, if necessary, fixes where he has not done well and where he has deviated from his goal. Although it is better not to make a mistake, it is worse not to act for fear of making that mistake. It is good to think before acting, but sometimes also after having acted, avoiding the two extremes of the one who acts and then thinks, and the one who needs to think so much that he never finishes acting. Examining yourself, or examining your own conduct, is part of the fundamental aspect of ethical life of making your own life the object of reflection: "What am I doing in, or with, my life? What have I done?" I believe that this is a good practice that should be carried out on a daily basis. To do this, it is necessary to seek and protect a few moments of silence. It is beneficial to dedicate a few minutes a day to contemplation, dialogue, and reflection. If you do not take time to think and reflect on your life and on what is happening around you, it is difficult to know where your life is going, whether it is growing or shrinking, whether it is getting better or worse, and whether you are getting closer or further away from the project that allows you to become what you want to be.

In this line, *be diligent and fast in what can bring you closer to your project and be slow in what can take you away*. Sometimes you do the opposite: you are fast in what takes you away from the project and slow in what brings you closer to what you want to become. This is a bad strategy. Be diligent in carrying out everything that can contribute to realizing that project, and slow in doing or deciding anything that might push you away or distance you from the project you freely embraced. Indeed, "giving yourself time" is also important when you would like to throw away the project or the relationship you have given almost everything to for a prolonged period of time. In such situations, the appropriate and prudent thing to do is to give yourself time.

We must not be discouraged: *"Don't give up!"*. Paul of Tarsus vividly experienced his own limitations and weakness and summarized his experience in the following question: "Why, wanting to do the good that I desire, do the evil that I do not desire?" St Paul's text is a beautiful way of recognizing our own weakness, which becomes clear when we decide to do something and then do not do it, or when we decide to stop doing something and end up doing it. It is a sign that our freedom is fragile. This can lead to either discouragement or to the decision to continue advancing in order to conquer new spaces of freedom. It is better to opt for the latter. In any case, it is a human experience, which St. Paul also experienced in an intense way after his conversion and articulated in a beautiful way almost two thousand years ago.

Sometimes we tend to procrastinate and put off the things that should be done, and then we experience a feeling of discomfort because of the mismatch between the task to be done and the time available. Hasn't everyone experienced a certain frustration when wanting to do something but lacking the courage to do it? We then see ourselves as useless, incapable and weak. Weakness is shown when we fail to do what we would like to do, or fail to stop doing what we would like to stop doing. Procrastination is a sign of this weakness: we would like to do something, but we lack the will-power to start and just get on with it. Everyone must discover their own strategies or techniques. I apply the Spanish saying that "the best defense is a good offense", and try to do the things that cost me the most first, as the more I delay them, the more they cost me. Trying to do the most burdensome things first is a good strategy.

On the other hand, sometimes we would like to do good, but it goes wrong. In cases where the result does not match the effort to do good, we should keep calm. When we try to do good but it goes wrong, nothing happens. The important thing is to have tried to do good. This has already made me a better person, regardless of the result or the fruit of the action. We need to acknowledge this, because otherwise our happiness would depend on factors beyond our control and leave us imprisoned by the feelings of fear and anguish that are so common in our society. This leads to a utilitarian vision, which contradicts the moral principle of doing good for love, rather than for a specific result. When we enter this utilitarian mentality, we end up reasoning in the following way: "Since this can go wrong for me, then it is better not to do it". This is a fatal mistake: we should want the good that we can, even if the result is not guaranteed. It is better to try to help others than to not do so for fear of making a mistake or of not being able to help them effectively.

On one occasion someone asked me where they could find that person or that book that can guide them in a moment of need or discouragement. I thought it was a good question. I answered that, although having a good person or book to trust is valuable, they are hard to find. The important thing is to keep searching and trying again and again. It is difficult not to achieve something when we are determined to do so. The problem is that we get tired after a few attempts and give up. Do not give up trying. *Do not give up!*

3) There is a time for everything: organize yourself. As Ecclesiastes 3 says, "[e]everything has its due time; there is a time for everything under heaven: a time to be born and a time to die; a time to plant and a time to harvest. . .". Therefore, organize yourself and put everything in order, because not everything has the same relevance in relation to your personal project. When organizing your time, it is important to keep in mind who you are and who you want to be, because this allows you to decide which things are more important than others. Logically, it is worth remembering something that was already said in chapter 2: people come first. Putting things before personal relationships is a sign that the project's content or its realization is failing. Time is necessary for all valuable things, and the most valuable things are ourselves and others. Therefore, friendship requires time; loving relationships (rather than merely superficial ones) grow deeper with time. Spend time cultivating and caring for human relationships, starting with your closest friends and family, while remaining open to meeting and building relationships with others. Building relationships with others is the thing that enriches us most and helps us grow as people.

4) Live and focus on the present, doing one thing after another. It is not easy to live completely in the present. We tend to think about what we have already done, what we should have done, or what we will have to do later. Try to recognize this tendency and try to put all your senses and powers into what you want or should do at each moment. Discover the things or thoughts that distract you, stress you, and get rid of them or ignore them. Otherwise, you will never be able to enjoy the present. It is important to live in the present with peace and joy. This is not possible if you cannot manage the flow of thoughts that wear you down mentally and stop you focusing on what is in front of you. You must get rid of them or ignore them. Once you have decided what you must do, try to focus exclusively on that. Only when you finish that task should you focus on the next. Do not get distracted by something that is not the right thing to do at that moment.

Each person has their own way of being and their own particular circumstances. It is true that controlling the mind is not easy, and that the tendency to become distracted is part of human frailty. In addition, certain circumstances can make it even more difficult: the uncertainty of the future, the fear of disappointing the people around us, and the fear of failure, especially when this has been caused by certain experiences we have gone through. All these thoughts can threaten our peace. It is important, first, to acknowledge these thoughts, and see if there is a good reason behind them. Sometimes they may be partly right, but generally they are created by our own imaginations, so we must get rid of them or ignore them because they impede our progress and prevent us from living in the present with peace. We can get rid of these thoughts in the same way that we manage other negative thoughts. If an insulting or slanderous thought against someone else crosses your mind, what do you do? You try to reject it or let it go immediately because that thought does not belong to you. The same should be done with other negative thoughts, without allowing ourselves to be trapped by them. These thoughts are offensive to ourselves, harmful, and must be rejected immediately so that we can focus on what truly matters to us. In the same way that the best defense is a good offense, we should not limit ourselves to rejecting negative or toxic thoughts; we must also actively engage with what the present asks of us.

Reacting in this way generally works. However, you may have to try harder, and with stronger negative thoughts it may even be advisable to speak with a professional. Before resorting to professional help, though, you should genuinely make the effort. The problem is that sometimes we do not realize how harmful these thoughts are, and therefore we do not reject them. As a result, they become more deeply rooted in our minds. This is a mistake. We must deal with them immediately or apply the old saying 'Ignoring someone is the strongest form of contempt' to our thoughts: we must ignore them completely.

We should also be careful when talking to people who have negative thoughts. We cannot change these people, but we can change the way we react when dealing with them. We must be realistic and positive in everything that depends on ourselves, even though our own environment may be negative or somewhat toxic. If we try to not let ourselves be infected by the bad, we are already improving the environment. But we should also not forget that we are responsible only for our own lives, not those of others. It is good to try to help, but we cannot carry a moral responsibility that belongs to others on our own shoulders.

In short, focus on the present, removing everything that distracts you. When you achieve this, you will perform better, you will get less tired, and you will start to enjoy what you are doing...

5) Take the appropriate time to do things: control impatience and anxiety. It is not a matter of falling into perfectionism, nor of letting oneself be carried away by a stringent attitude when doing what you must do. It is good to be diligent and decisive. But it is important not to forget that things require a minimum amount of time. Trying to do things in less time or at a faster pace may be efficient in the short and medium term from a professional and pragmatic perspective, but not in the long term, and it is certainly harmful to personal growth. As has been said, contemplation, reflection and dialogue are actions that are at odds with haste, recklessness, and impatience. "Zamora was not conquered in an hour." Each thing has its time or moment, as has been said, but it also requires time. Beware of wanting to do and finish things too quickly! There is a danger that they will not be done well, and they will not do good to the person who does them that way. Frequently, mental illnesses or disorders such as anxiety or depression come from doing things too quickly too often. Impatience is a cancer that should be eradicated. Otherwise, it grows and causes havoc with time.

As has been said, one of the keys to living, focusing and enjoying the present consists in doing one thing after another, each thing in its own time. When we try to do things too quickly, it is difficult to enjoy what we are doing. If we try to do things faster to achieve more in less time, we start to not enjoy them and ultimately burn ourselves out. We can live like this for a while, but it is important not to abuse this resource, even when we do have the capacity to do it.

There are people with an excessively prompt or decisive character, who seek efficiency above all else (*"getting things done"*). What is the problem with this attitude? It prevents the cultivation of the three fundamental sources of knowledge. The first and most important is the contemplation of reality. If you drive along the highway at three hundred kilometers per hour, you can only see the ground and the lines that mark the road; you cannot think about anything. However, if you drive more slowly, ride a bicycle or walk in the countryside, you can observe the landscape and capture its details, like the songs of the birds, the smell of the flowers, and the color of the leaves of the trees. You can enjoy reality, while at the same time reflecting and conversing. Living too quickly desensitizes us, because it makes us think that the only things that are worthwhile are those that result in efficiency, productivity, and profitability.

Machines can be programmed for this, but are not human. This way of living prevents both contemplation and reflection. It also impedes dialogue: sometimes we do not have time to be with our family and friends and to talk to them, and we can even come to think that this is a waste of time. The current trend is to "humanize" machines and robotize human beings, adopting the time unit of the nanosecond. If something can be done in fewer seconds, the better – there is more productivity and more profitability. This mentality is dehumanizing because it prevents us from developing those great rational or intellectual capacities that characterize and define human beings: contemplating reality, reflecting and dialoguing.

Therefore, high speed is best left for trains and other machines. Perhaps it may be important at a given moment (for example, for those about to sit an exam or for those facing a busy period at work) but living habitually at that speed or going through life against the clock, results in us sliding down a path that ends up impoverishing, depersonalizing and dehumanizing those who take it. We can do many things, but they are of little use if that efficiency distances us from what characterizes and defines us as people, and if it does not bring us closer to what we truly want to become. Becoming more human requires us to develop our capacities for contemplation, reflection and dialogue. Otherwise, we become a stranger to both ourselves and others.

6) **Do not reduce your personal project to specific results or objectives**. As has been said, you are worth much more than results, fruits or objectives in life. Confusing or identifying a personal project with certain objectives is a serious mistake. A personal project is much more than the attainment of certain achievements. It is true that some objectives can serve as milestones or reference points along the way, but if it is not possible to achieve them, it is worth remembering the saying that "where one door closes, another one opens". The project is still there, unscathed, and you must continue. The passage of time often shows that the objective was not so important or, even if it was, the lack of "success" brought even greater goods. Life has a mysterious dimension that time is in charge of revealing or unraveling, but it is important to be patient and not to succumb to discouragement.

7) **Be strong. Grow in the face of difficulties**. No one is born strong; one becomes strong. And this depends on each person's decisions and conduct. Adversity helps us to grow and become stronger; going against the tide helps you to become what you want to become. Life has taught me this. Now, if I notice that I am doing something that everyone else is doing, I ask myself if I am doing something wrong. I cannot resist transcribing here four rules or criteria that Ortega y Gasset recommended back in 1928, to young people, although they are of equal relevance to adults:

> "1st Never pay attention to what people think. People are all those crowds that surround you—at home, at school, at University, in friendship groups, in Parliament, in public, and in the newspapers. Observe and you will notice that these people never know why they say what they say, they do not prove their opinions, and they judge by passion rather than by reason.
>
> 2nd It follows from the first rule that you should never let yourself be swayed by the opinions of others. Try

to convince *yourself*. The soul that thinks, feels and wants through the influence of others is a vile soul, which cannot think for itself.

3ʳᵈ To say of a man that he has true moral or intellectual value says that in his way of being or thinking he has risen above ordinary feeling and thinking. This makes his ways of being and thinking difficult to understand, and often they clash with that of the norm. We know, therefore, that the thing most valuable to us will seem strange, unusual or annoying at first.

4ᵗʰ In every struggle of ideas or feelings, when you see that many fight on one side and few on the other, suspect that the reason is in the latter. Nobly lend your help to the minority against the majority" (Text contained in the volume entitled *Nuestra raza*, handwritten school reading book. Editorial Hispano-Americana, Reus, 1928).

I have always been captivated by that fourth rule, applicable to ideas and ways of living: "when you see many fighting on one side and few on the other, suspect that the reason is in the latter". This does not mean we should have a spirit of contradiction, where we are always against everything. Sociology studies the tendency of human beings to mimic. After hearing a lie a hundred times, people tend to think that it is the truth. However, we should engage in critical thinking to prevent the conversion of something false into something true by mere repetition. You should say to yourself: "for me a lie will remain a lie, even if it is repeated millions of times. And if there are few people who think like me, this is a pity because I will not change or at least, I will try not to change".

8) Don't run away from yourself: seek and protect times of silence. Silence is absolutely essential to become someone through the course of time. It is important to seek and find time for silence, which is needed to contemplate reality, reflection and dialogue. The technological advances of the postmodern world have not succeeded in banishing something that began to flood cities after the industrial revolution: noise. It seems as if human beings are uncomfortable with silence. It is important to reconcile with silence, and to value it. Silence allows us to reconcile with ourselves, to get used to being with ourselves, to think calmly about things. Sometimes we might want to combine silence with the reading of a good text, or a conversation with a good friend, a partner, or a child.

There is a story in Greek mythology that tells how the gods gathered and decided what they could do to prevent human beings from becoming as happy as the gods. How can we make man unhappy and always wanting to be more, since the gods are happy while they are not? Aeolus, the god of the winds, appeared and said: I would put the treasure on the top of a very high peak that was very difficult to access, so that man could not find the treasure. Then Poseidon, the god of the sea, said: No, it would be better to put the treasure in the depths of the sea, since they would not be able to find it there. Zeus, god of the gods, intervened and said: No, they will look for it there too. Let us put happiness in the most intimate and deepest part of the human being. They will certainly not look for it there.

I think it is a big problem to live always turned towards what is happening outside us. The news is constantly accessible and constantly updating, so we can spend the entire day looking at what is happening all over the world. This tendency hinders the journey into oneself, which is the most important thing. It is there where the deepest freedom of the human being lies, from there also arises the recognition of ourselves and others, as well as the ability to communicate with others and understand them (even when some people do not facilitate it or do not manage to communicate well). From there, a gesture or a glance can be interpreted in depth. This sensitivity to ourselves, others, and the world around us comes largely from a capacity for contemplation and reflection. Developing this capacity requires silence. Without silence it is not possible to contemplate or reflect. Noise and movement are constant in today's society, which makes it difficult to communicate.

Beauty, truth and goodness are discovered with time: it is the result and reward of a calm and lasting contemplative attitude in time. Immediacy, instantaneity and transience may be very cool and emotional, but they leave no trace. In fact, they make us superficial because they sacrifice everything to the immediate and momentary. There is no time to live calmly, think calmly to try to get to the bottom of a question, to look slowly, to listen carefully, read carefully, or to build something that goes beyond today, connecting yesterday and tomorrow.

The truth manifests itself in silence or in a barely perceptible whisper. We must develop the ability to listen, which is often reduced by the interior and exterior noises around us. We must try to get out of a state of daze that makes us insensitive to the whisper of the beautiful, the good and the true. To live in a daze and with our senses dulled is easy; to increase our capacity to contemplate and listen to reality is more complex. And the excess of speed, noise and sensations make it even more difficult.

9) To strive in every task and relationship, and above all, to love. In reality, there is no stronger motivation or driving force than love. We want to love and to feel love. It is true that the stimulus and the aspiration that a good personal project usually generates can pull us forward, but there are radical or deep motivations that pull much more. Self-esteem, and more fundamentally love for others (and for God, for believers), has a much greater force. Doing something for the good of others stimulates our creative capacity and willingness to sacrifice ourselves for something that really deserves it. A better teacher is usually the one who appreciates and seeks the good of his students, and a better businessperson is the one who keeps in mind the good of his workers, suppliers and clients. It is not the case that love prevents us from taking advantage of time or fulfilling our obligations, it is merely that it causes us to act for more than just the mere fulfilment of a duty or for utilitarian reasons of efficiency. Love is always the most profitable thing for those who love, but it is not for those who are primarily driven by other more utilitarian motives.

There is a helpful saying: "If you want to fly, love and you will know what it is to fly". Love's crucial consequence is that it enables us to value the present, because it is only in the present that we can love. We can only live and strive for a full life in the present. This is a present that can be lived with different motivations, such as out of a sense of duty, for the desire to show up, or for "*getting things done*". The highest motivation for living a full life in the present, however, is undoubtably love. Consequently, the best way to live well in the present is to ensure that each and every act is done with love and for love. Love should be the driver behind what is done in every moment. Thus, we must concentrate on loving here and now, because love can only be given and received in the present moment. This also means that we should do things for the good of others, thinking of the service we are giving them. This is a fundamental condition for an authentic human life.

THE CHALLENGE OF THE PASSAGE OF TIME

Why does the passage of time present such a challenge to our own personal fulfillment? Because it puts us in reality. The passage of time questions and affects everyone, and it is only there that the consistency and coherence of our life project is put to the test. We can want many things, have great ideas, make intelligent decisions, make good intentions or pronounce beautiful words. These become more real when we can show that throughout time, they are not just words, ideas and decisions, but realities. And they are real because we can carry them out in a lasting and stable way, even in the face of difficulties. Time is, then, the test that allows us to distinguish the true from the false, the authentic from the imposters, the consistent from the fragile, and the reality from the mere desire.

To achieve a successful and fulfilled life, it is not enough to 1) know yourself, accept yourself and be grateful and 2) decide what you want to be through a personal project that gives priority to human relationships. Both are necessary, but not sufficient. It is necessary 3) to carry out this project over time, overcoming the illusion of the immediate and ephemeral. There is much talk of sustainability, without realizing how impossible it is for a society focused on the momentary to constitute something lasting in time. What is fleeting, transitory and immediate cannot be, at the same time, stable and lasting, just as the extraordinary ceases to be extraordinary when it is the norm. It would be quite another thing, however, to do the ordinary in an extraordinary way, where we try and do it in the best possible way.

In order to achieve this long-lasting project, it is important to keep in mind and apply some of the ideas and keys described here. Putting them into practice requires, especially to start with, a little effort to cultivate and acquire a set of stable tendencies or habits (or 'virtues', as Aristotle began to call them), which are necessary for us to complete the personal project we have proposed. Carry out that project that excited you and led you to make a decision you committed your entire life to. Do not allow the passage of time to erase it, like the tide erases the words of love written on the shore.

CHAPTER 4

FOUR ETHICAL PRINCIPLES
FOR A FREE AND MATURE SOCIETY

ETHICS, HUMAN HAPPINESS, AND SOCIAL JUSTICE

I have never met anyone who has renounced happiness. I have never met anyone who has given up any kind of ethics in order to achieve happiness. In fact, there is a clear link between an ethical life and a happy life. The connection between ethics and happiness is a permanent feature in scholarship, from Greek philosophy to the present day.

Is it possible to be happy in isolation from others? Can we be happy when the people around us are unhappy? Is it possible? At first glance, it seems difficult to be happy when the people around us are not happy. It seems that my happiness is at least partially dependent on the happiness of the people around me.

Democritus, a pre-Socratic thinker, stated that "he who commits injustice is more unfortunate than he who suffers it".[1]

1. Text n. 759 (68 B 45), Democritus, 11 (collected in *Los filósofos presocráti-cos* (Introductions, translations and notes by A. Poratti, C.E. Lan, M.I. Santa Cruz de Prunes and N.L. Cordero), Madrid: Gredos, 1986 (https://archive.org/stream/ColeccionObrasGrecoLatinas1/028.losFilsofosPresocrticosIii_djvu.txt); read other statements of Democritus on human goodness: text n. 755 (68 B 48) Democritus, 14: "The good man does not stop to think about the insults of insignificant people"; text n. 755 (68 B 48) Democritus, 14: "The good man does not stop to think about the insults of insignificant people", 14: "The good

Even though today's mentality may lead us to think that it is the opposite, his statement remains true.

Aristotle said that we call just "that which is of this nature to produce and preserve happiness and its elements for the political community".[2] Therefore, **Aristotle** connects justice (which should be linked to ethics) to happiness, and then he connects happiness to the whole of the political community. This connection between ethics, happiness and justice leads us to the following great question: Is an ethical society possible?

My answer is a resounding YES. It is not only possible, but necessary. **Aristotle**, when referring to the elements of happiness for the political community, argued that there are three goods that lead to happiness: virtue, prudence, and pleasure.[3] Today, there is a widespread idea that the fundamental element of happiness is pleasure. The greater the pleasure, the greater the happiness: this is the core of utilitarian philosophy, which has influenced modern thinking. However, for Aristotle, the core of happiness was virtue, the quality that results from acting in the right way, while also helping us act in the right way in the future.[4] He said that this is because virtue is "that way of being that makes us capable of

man does not dwell on the insults of insignificant people"; text n. 756 (68 B 39) Democritus, 4: "It is beautiful to prevent someone from committing injustice; and if that is not possible, at least not to become an accomplice"; text n. 757 (68 B 39) Democ., 5: "One should be good, or else imitate the one who is good"; text n. 758 (68 B 43) Democ, 9: "To repent of evil deeds is the salvation of life"; text n. 760 (68 B 62) Democ., 27: "It is good not so much not to commit injustice, as not to intend to commit injustice"; text n. 761 (68 B 89) Democ., 55: "Detestable is not he who commits injustice, but he who does it deliberately."

2. Aristotle, *Nicomachean Ethics*, V, 1, 1129 b18–20.

3. Aristotle, *Eudemian Ethics* 1218b32; happiness, therefore, is associated with three genres of life: the political life (it is concerned with noble actions, those that flow from virtue), the philosophical life or "contemplative life" (it is concerned with prudence and the contemplation of truth), and the life of pleasure or "voluptuous life" (it is concerned with enjoyment and bodily pleasures) (Aristotle, *Eudemian Ethics1215a33–1215b1–4*).

4. Aristotle, *Eudemian Ethics* 1220a30–32.

performing the best acts and that disposes us as well as possible to a better good or act, which is in accordance with right reason".[5]

Thomas Aquinas argued that justice required every ruler to aim to safeguard the common good and try to achieve the welfare of his subjects. Moreover, he said that the happiness and welfare of society as a whole is somehow related to public governance, because the ruler must aim at safeguarding the common good. The law helps to do this by providing a tool the ruler can manage the public with. He defined law as "a prescription of reason for the common good, promulgated by the one who has the care of the community".[6] I do not want to dwell now on the reference to the 'prescription of reason',[7] but I do want to emphasize the expression 'in order to the common good'. This is the need for a public power to have recourse to laws that contribute to the public good and therefore facilitate the achievement of happiness for society as a whole. This idea is recurrent in the history of medieval and modern thought, passing through industrialization (17th century), the Enlightenment (18th century), and continuing to the present day.

The connection between justice, ethics and happiness has found its way into legal texts, particularly in constitutions. The *American Declaration of Independence* (July 4, 1776), for example, contains express references to inalienable rights such as the rights to life, liberty and to the pursuit of happiness. This text was largely derived from the earlier *Declaration of Virginia*, which mentions the existence of certain innate rights, such as life, liberty, and property, as well as the pursuit of happiness and security. It was clearly influenced by the work of **John Locke**.

5. Aristotle, *Ética Eudemia* 1222a8; in this regard, see, for example, Luis Fernando Garcés Giraldo, "La virtud aristotélica como camino de excelencia humana y las acciones para alcanzarla", *Discusiones Filosóficas*, año 16 n° 27, julio—diciembre 2015. pp. 127–146 (http://www.scielo.org.co/pdf/difil/v16n27/v16n27a08.pdf).

6. Thomas Aquinas, *Summa Theologica*, I, II, c. 90, a. 4.

7. This is despite the relevance of the 'prescription of reason', especially when modern thought substitutes reason for will, conceiving law more as a mandate of the State than as a requirement of reason. Modern thought appeals more to coerciveness than to reason.

The relationship between public governance and happiness also appears in the *Declaration of the Rights of Man and the Citizen* of 1789, a text that linked our inalienable natural rights to human happiness. This text was incorporated into the *French Constitution* of 1791, which reproduced the paragraph of the *Declaration*. Two years later, the *French Constitution* of 1793 stated in its first article that "the end of society is the common happiness. Government is instituted to guarantee man the enjoyment of his natural and undeniable rights".

Let us now move from the American and French context to the Spanish one. The *Constitution of Bayonne*, of July 1808, required the king to "govern only with a view to the interest, happiness and glory of the Spanish nation" (art. 6). Four years later, the *Cadiz Constitution of* 1812 stated that "the object of the Government is the happiness of the nation, since the purpose of any political society is none other than the welfare of the individuals who compose it" (art. 13).

After analyzing the close relationship between social justice, ethics, and happiness, we should ask again: is an ethical society possible? You could always argue that it would be possible if the rulers allowed it or created minimum conditions for it. It is undeniable that the realization of an ethical society would be easier if public authorities governed with the aim of the common good and the nation's happiness, using just laws. This is true, but my thesis is that this goal is a task for society as a whole, so it is possible to achieve an ethical society even when the rulers do little to contribute to this.[8]

John S. Mill wondered what would happen if society reached a point where everyone had work, a home, education, and health care. And he asked: even if the State achieved all this, would the individual truly be happy? He concluded NO, because happiness does not depend only on material comfort, although it is necessary and helpful. In fact, it is said that he spent a few days depressed

---

8. Aniceto Masferrer, "Is a humanizing regeneration of society and politics possible?", *Para una nueva cultura política*, Madrid: Catarata, 2019, pp. 11–15.

when he realized that even if political power is used well, it cannot guarantee the happiness of all individuals in the community.

Happiness is a personal conquest, but we can benefit from the help of others. It is related to ethics. And ethics is not merely a set of rules or regulations that have been derived from certain criteria, such as Kantian duty. Rather, ethics is a set of fundamental maxims of human behavior and many of them have to do with other people, and with "the constant and perpetual will to give to each one what is his own" (**Ulpianus**),[9] so that we may each have a full, successful, and happy life. There is, therefore, a direct connection between both ethics and the happiness of each person, and between those and justice and social welfare.

ETHICS AND FREEDOM

At this point, it is useful to discuss some preliminary ideas on ethics before describing a series of fundamental keys to an ethical life in the last part.

The first fundamental idea is freedom. Freedom is a key concept: it is a fundamental necessity to lead an ethical life. The person who understands ethics as a set of normative prescriptions does not lead a healthy moral life, because the focus is on conforming to these prescriptions, rather than freely understanding

---

9. It can also be translated as "the perpetual and constant will to give to each one his right". Let us look at the complete text: "The precepts of the law are: to live honestly, to harm no one and to give to each one what is his" (*Iuris praecepta sunt haec: honeste vivere, alterum non laedere, suum cuique tribuere*, D.1.1.10.1). Similar definitions of justice can be found in Cicero ("Justice is a habit of the soul, which observed in the common interest gives to each his dignity"), Aristotle (whose theory of justice appears in his *Ethics to Nicomacheus*, Book IV. For Aristotle, justice is a virtue that seeks the good of others, EN 1129b—1130a; Consequently, the best man, the most just, is not the one who uses the virtues for his own benefit, but for the benefit of others, EN 1129b 30), and Thomas Aquinas (for whom justice is "the habit according to which one, with constant and perpetual will, gives to each one his right", *Summa Theologica*, II-II, q. 58, a. 1), and Thomas Aquinas (for whom justice is "the habit according to which one, with constant and perpetual will, gives to each one his right", *Summa Theologica*, II-II, q. 58, a. 1). 58, a. 1).

and wisely choosing how to live. And this is so because moral life must be lived in freedom. Moreover, that person would not be happy because, fundamentally, morality does not exist in the fulfillment of rules. Therefore, we must recognize the crucial fact that freedom depends mostly on what I do: no one can do it for me. Let me explain. If I let someone else act for me, then I do not reach that fullness of life. To reach this fullness we must act freely, not because someone else has told us to do so or because there is a regulation that demands us to act in a certain way. To make sense of moral maxims, we should grasp at them with reason before choosing to adhere to them. We need to grasp the meaning of moral maxims. Once we do, we feel drawn to them and begin to embrace them freely. This is how we become good—not by merely submitting to rules whose purpose we do not understand.

Therefore, I insist that in order to be happy, we must exercise freedom. In fact, freedom is precisely what makes us moral beings. We would not be moral beings if we did not have freedom. There is a direct connection between freedom and the moral dimension of the person. We must, therefore, make decisions that make us freer. There are decisions that contribute to this, but also decisions that diminish, restrict, or subtract freedom from the person who makes them. To achieve happiness, we must conquer the freedom that is necessary for us to live fully.

This requires effort. However, most importantly it requires, as **Aristotle** said, prudence. It requires the ability to understand, to see how I can apply a fundamental moral maxim in a specific context, in specific circumstances and in relation to a specific person. Moreover, virtue and pleasure also play their part. When freedom is exercised well, with the passage of time there comes a time where we begin to enjoy doing what is good. This itself is a good thing.

Therefore, the first fundamental idea for a moral life is freedom. We can only be morally good if we start with freedom. This is a simple idea in theory, but not in practice.

The second idea is that this freedom must be taken seriously. We live only one life. That life is unique and can never be repeated by another. Even if the connection between friends or between members of a family makes their experiences similar, their lives nonetheless remain unique.

Moreover, we should not be afraid of originality, distinguishing ourselves from others, or being ourselves. Freedom carries with it a radical mandate: "Be yourself". Live your life, rather than someone else's life, or how others would live in your position. Society needs your uniqueness, your way of being, your way of thinking, your way of behaving, your personality, and your autobiography. Only you can offer that to society, to your country and to the whole world.

That can sometimes be scary in a world where it seems that we all tend to be very similar. This can make it frightening to be unique and not like everyone else. For this I refer to **Kant's** book *An Answer to the Question: What is Enlightenment?*, written in 1784, where he writes that there are two great obstacles one must overcome: laziness and cowardice. These are the main barriers that prevent us from maturing and developing. You might mistakenly think that it is better not to complicate life, not to single yourself out, and not to put effort into what is worthwhile, and instead be satisfied by instant gratification and rapidly changing desires.

How often we suffer from the fear of not reaping the fruit of what we have sown! We worry that the effort we put into something may be in vain. It is an understandable fear, but a wrong one. It is a mistake to focus primarily on the outcome when making decisions. Making decisions fundamentally on the basis of the result, rather than on the goodness in itself of what you want to achieve, weakens your moral life. It is a source of anguish and anxiety, because if you do not achieve that result, the effort put in feels pointless.

Moreover, in today's society everything goes so fast that we want things immediately. Where we cannot do this, the act feels like a waste of time. We see ourselves as inefficient compared to those who can reap immediate results. Sometimes we focus too much on what is obvious when, as **Antoine de Saint-Exupéry** says, "what is essential is invisible to the eye."[10] Generally, the most important things are those that cannot be seen. Sometimes we tend to look for the big or the obvious. We get discouraged when we see that a result will not be achieved quickly, or if it seems too small or insignificant.

That is why sometimes we get lazy and question the point of doing something. Often cowardice also has to do with fear. There is a lot of fear throughout our society: the fear of failing, the fear of not living up to what the people around us expect of us, the fear of looking bad, the fear of being rejected, the fear of being different, and the fear of not being understood. This prevents us from being happy and from being ourselves. I advise you to follow **Kant** in his work *What Is Enlightenment?*: "Sapere aude".[11] "Dare to know": dare to think for yourself, dare to discern what is good from what is not, think for yourself and do not let yourself be paralyzed by laziness and cowardice.

FOUR ETHICAL PRINCIPLES TO ESTABLISH A FREE AND MATURE SOCIETY

Just as there are four fundamental principles to the ethical regeneration of those who dedicate themselves to public affairs[12], there are, in my opinion, four others which apply to the contribution of every citizen to the ethical flourishing of society.

The ethics of a country or society is, to a large extent, the sum of the ethical life of the individuals that make it up. If you try to be better, you are already improving society as a whole. Sometimes we could become depressed when seeing things as they are. We would like to be the savior or the messiah of the world we live in, but this is not possible. We have to live in reality.

10. Antoine de Saint-Exupéry, *The Little Prince* (1943), ch. 21: "One can only see with the heart. What is essential is invisible to the eyes".

11. See footnote 14.

12. Aniceto Masferrer, "Regeneración política", *Para una nueva cultura política*, Madrid: Catarata, 2019, pp. 17–20.

What we can do is to live better and improve as people; living this way always has a contagious effect. Even if the effect is not immediately visible, living better builds a more ethical society. It is true that if everyone did a little more of this, society as a whole would improve. We would live better, it would be a fairer society that may be less competitive and more collaborative, and we would help each other more.

Let us now look at the four ethical principles which have a collective effective and benefit society as a whole.[13]

1st) Thinking for yourself

The first principle is key: think for yourself. This is a fundamental principle of moral living. Do not let others think for you. You cannot be yourself if you do this. Letting others think for you leads to them acting and making decisions for you as well. This is the opposite of an ethical life, because an ethical life requires the deep, real, and authentic exercise of personal freedom.

Blaise Pascal said that the purpose of morality is "to strive to think well."[14] Because the purpose of morality is not to allow us to comply with a series of specific rules of conduct, it does not require us to have a great memory. No. There are fundamental moral principles that can be shared by millions of people regardless of their cultural or religious tradition, and we can succeed in determining what is good if we exercise reason and really stop and think for ourselves.

John Finnis argued that in order to make good decisions, we must overcome three obstacles: culture, interest, and passion.[15]

---

13. All of them, among others, are collected in a more exhaustive way, in the *Manual de ética para la vida moderna*, Madrid: Edaf, 2020.

14. "Strive to think well; here is the principle of morality," is the full statement that can be found, in addition to the internet, in Blaise Pascal, *Pensamientos, opúsculos, cartas*, Madrid: Gredos, 2012.

15. John Finnis, "Is natural law theory compatible with limited government?", in Robert P. George, Natural law, Liberalism and Morality, Oxford: Oxford University Press, 1996, pp. 1–26, whose fundamental thesis of the chapter could be summarized in the following statement: "In any sound theory

Regarding culture, we tend to take the ideas that are deeply embedded in our social mentality for granted. The tendency to take almost everything for granted is dangerous. One key example is 19th century America, where the 'rightness' of racism and slavery was taken for granted. How could they live without slaves? The fact that slavery was so deeply embedded in that culture did not make it a morally good thing. This shows that culture can sometimes be an obstacle to overcome. It requires the minority to think for themselves and reach conclusions that differ from those of the majority. This is especially so where the majority view is created by lobbyists, who use their financial, political or ideological influence to collude with the media to shape majority thinking.

The second obstacle is self-interest. When we have a very intense interest in something, it is difficult to think in an impartial way, which causes us to make the decision that benefits our personal interests. This means that we should be cautious when it comes to our personal interests, because they can prevent us from having a realistic vision and from making fair decisions. A citizen who is concerned about public affairs is not the same as a politician whose role is public affairs. Making a moral decision on something you have a personal interest in is not the same as making a decision on something you have no interest in.

The third obstacle is passion. We all have passions; it is human to have them, and they are certainly not bad in themselves. Some passions lead us to do great good, while others do not. The force of passion demands a free and conscious response. This requires turning to reason to determine whether following that passion is good or bad. This is self-control, or self-determination. The Kantian *sapere aude* is applicable here: dare to think and to overcome obstacles.[16] Experience can be a valuable aid for moral life. Bad

of natural law, the authority of government is explained and justified as an authority limited by positive law (. . . .), by the moral principles and norms of justice which apply to all human action (. . .), and by the common good of political communities-a common good which I shall argue he is inherently instrumental and therefore limited" (p. 1).

16. As is well known, the expression *Sapere aude* ("Dare to know"), included in the Kantian text *What is Enlightenment?* (1784), was taken from Epistle

decisions of the past can help us to react and to realize what is good and the bad experiences of others also teach us. Sometimes even reading a good book can help to guide us. However, nothing should ever replace our own critical thinking and personal reflection.

2nd) Expressing your thoughts

The second idea has a lot to do with the first principle: express what you think. There would be little point in a person thinking, reflecting and developing his own views on what he thinks an ethical and healthy life is if he was not allowed to express these views in public. It would be a mistake. Show yourself as you are and express what you think. This is demanded by the first principle. Moreover, we only know what we think when we express it. Personal thought is not fully formed until it is expressed. It can be expressed internally, but it helps a lot to verbalize it by speaking, writing and talking to other people.

Gandhi said that "happiness is achieved when what one thinks, says and does is in harmony". We should all subscribe to this: there is harmony between what we think, say and do. Hypocrisy is the opposite of a good ethical life. Sometimes we should be prudent and not to say everything we think. But there are limits to this – if you habitually live under the guise of supposed prudence, you do not live in harmony with what you think, say and do. This does not contribute to a happy or successful life.

Therefore, the first thing to do is to think or reason. However, this is not enough. We must acquire the habit of being able to express what we think. I need harmony and coherence to conquer the freedom that allows me to lead a happy life, so I must reject hypocrisy and falsehood. A person who does live a life of hypocrisy

---

II (*Epistularumliber primus*), by the poet Horace, written to his friend Lolius in the first century B.C. in the following terms: *Dimidiumfacti, qui coepit, habet: sapere aude, / incipe* ("He who has begun, has already done half: dare to know, begin").

will have to change and get closer to that harmony between what he thinks, says and does.

3ʳᵈ) Respect and seek the good of others

Logically, this should not be done by not disrespecting others, which brings us to the **third point: respect and seek the good of others.** Respect for others requires openness and love, seeking the good of the other, whom I need to know to recognize myself. We must not only respect others, but say to them: "I not only respect you because I see myself in you, but because you are part of me, and we need each other to enrich ourselves" (and you enrich me the most when you think differently to me, as this helps me to think). It follows from the need to respect others that we must add the positive want to do as much good to them as we can. This is a fundamental ethical maxim: "Do as much good as you can to others".

Aristotle thought that man is a political animal,[17] and **Victor Frankl** argued that the doors of happiness open outwards.[18] Indeed, the doors of happiness do open outwards; they lead to openness to others, rather than withdrawal. Otherwise, we fall into the views of existentialist philosophers such as **Sartre**, who thought that "hell is others," who limit and humiliate me with their judgment, and that we must judge others to know ourselves.[19]

17. Aristotle, *Politics*, I. 1253a 2–8: "From all this it is evident that the city is one of the natural things, and that man is by nature a social animal, and that the unsocial by nature and not by chance is either an inferior being or a superior being to man."

18. Victor Frankl, *Man's Search for Meaning* (1946); a statement that the Austrian psychiatrist made as a counterpoint to that of the Danish philosopher Søren Kierkegaard, who considered that the door opened inwards ("The door to happiness opens inwards, you have to withdraw a little to open it: if you push, it closes more and more").

19. Jean-Paul Sartre, *A puerta cerrada*, Madrid: Alianza, 1981; see the original French version, Jean-Paul Sartre, *Huis clos—L'enfer c'est les autres*, FrémeauxColombini SAS, 2010 (available at https://www.philo5.com/Les%20 philosophes%20Textes/Sartre_L'EnferC'EstLesAutres.htm#_ftn1): "They have always misunderstood "Hell is others". They have believed that by this they

We must cultivate a culture of respect. This also means engaging in listening and dialogue, especially with those who think differently, and accepting others without judging them. Looking at people with good eyes is a way of treating them with respect, without labeling or instrumentalizing them. To move from respect to help or to seek their good is, in essence, to love. To love a person is to seek the best for him or her and to seek his or her good. Even though this may go beyond my own personal interests, a successful life leaves no one behind. The good of others ultimately ends up becoming one of my own interests.

4th) Seek excellence in everything we do

The fourth point refers to another ethical maxim: strive for excellence in everything you do. What you do encompasses everything: study, work, family life, social life, dealing with friends, and hobbies. It is about trying to do everything you do or have to do well. This is another fundamental ethical maxim. It might seem that this principle does not fit with the criticism of the person who seeks only the immediate and the result. Not at all. He who seeks excellence does not pursue the result, but the good. This is the reason why he strives to work in an excellent way. You should try to do everything that seems like it can create good for you and others, even if it is tough and complicated (as long as it will not break you

---

meant that our relationships with others were always poisoned and that they were always hellish relationships. And yet, what I mean is something quite different. I mean that if our relations with the other are twisted, vitiated, then the other can only be hell. Why? Because the others are the most important thing in ourselves and for our own knowledge of ourselves. When we reflect on ourselves, when we try to know ourselves. We basically use knowledge that others already have about us, and we judge ourselves with the means that others have to judge us. The judgment of others always enters into what I have to say and feel about myself. This means that if my relationships are bad, I place myself in total dependence on the other and then, in effect, I am in hell. And there are many people in the world who are in hell because they are too dependent on the judgment of others. But that does not at all mean that we cannot have other relationships with others, it simply points out the capital importance of all others for each one of us".

internally, of course; it is up to each one of us to see how far our strength can go and the mental stamina we have).

Acting in a good conscience by doing what we believe we must do (because we perceive it as good) when we know we might not get the expected result has an incredibly positive effect on us. Why? Because the fundamental criterion of ethics is neither utilitarian nor pragmatic. The search for the result in everything usually generates tension, anguish, anxiety, or depression.

In the pursuit of excellence, be creative and authentic; do good and try to do everything well. I insist: strive to spend your life doing good and doing things well. These are different things. Try to discover, with both mind and heart, how to do good and how to do things well—but do not act merely out of interest, recognition, or reward. Although it is better to do good for a reward than not to do good at all, if you want to build a successful, deep, and authentic life, you should try to act for the sake of the good itself. Only in this way do you become good and grow as a person. This is so because you become what you seek through your actions and behavior. As Aristotle says, the reward of virtue is virtue itself—and it is virtue that brings happiness.

Let me give you an example. Imagine you are on the street, and you see a person at a traffic light who offers to help the blind man standing next to them cross the street: "Would you like me to help you cross the street? The blind man agrees, and they cross the street together. What would you think? "What a nice act!". The blind man walks down the street and comes to another crossing, and the same thing happens with another person who assists him. The two acts appear identical: a person in need is helped by someone who can make it easier for him to cross the street. However, the two acts may be completely different if the motives behind the acts are different. Perhaps the first person has given that help because he wanted to look good in front a person nearby, whereas the other person has done it simply because he wanted to help the blind person, regardless of whether he looks good or bad. These two people have been developed by why they have sought to act. If you wanted to act well and were looking for ways to help the blind person, you would become good by rendering that service. If you have sought to look good, you will have only appeared good rather than becoming a better person. This especially because morality has to do with truth and good, not with appearance, hypocrisy or falsehood.

FINAL CONSIDERATION

It is up to the reader to determine how accurate the thesis put forward here is, namely, that the ethical flourishing of a society does not fundamentally depend on its rulers, but on the personal ethics of its citizens as a whole. What would happen if the majority were obliged to put into practice the four principles analyzed here? Let us mention them again here, as a reminder and by way of conclusion: 1st) Think for oneself; 2nd) Express freely (and respectfully) what one thinks; 3rd) Respect and seek the good of others; and 4th) Seek excellence in everything one does.

My answer to the question is clear: the greatest social revolution ever seen would take place. It would not be a violent revolution, but a peaceful and lasting one. This is because it would be based truly on ethical individuals living in freedom, potentially in spite of the rulers, who themselves would have to change if they wished to continue governing. We would be facing an authentic and truly mature democracy, where everyone would contribute – with their lives, their work and their active participation through the exercise of freedom of expression in the processes of public deliberation – to the flourishing of a freer and more mature society.

Epilogue

LIVING IN FREEDOM IS A LEARNED SKILL

I DO NOT WANT to end this book without addressing the younger reader (perhaps the student who would like to know how and where to start after reading the book) more directly. I would also like to address the teacher who would like to contribute more positively to the process of growth and maturation of their students, but is aware of the magnitude of this task. To both, it is important to say that we are not born knowing how to live freely or how to be a good teacher, but we learn it. This is not something that is given to you, but something that you learn. This learning depends above all, and beyond the educational system or working conditions, on yourself.

"I DON'T CHEAT YOU": LETTER FROM
A UNIVERSITY PROFESSOR TO HIS STUDENT

Dear student, I recently read a letter from a colleague of mine, a professor of another discipline and university, in which he confessed to his undergraduate student that he was cheating him. Actually, it included more professors: "We are cheating you." After reading it with interest and reflecting on it, I feel an obligation to confess that I, unlike that colleague of mine, have never cheated you. In fact, my teaching experience over the course of a quarter of a century has been quite different. I would be lying if I said that things have not changed in recent years. Your preparation is noticeably worse than it was a decade ago: it is much harder for you to read a text, to try to understand it, and to reflect and to express your ideas orally and in writing. In addition, you have greater difficulty in concentrating and maintaining attention. This is evident and you experience it daily.

However, at the same time, I see your eagerness to improve and excel, your non-conformist yearning, and your interest and curiosity to learn. For me it is a repeated miracle to see how you keep your attention for an hour and a half or two hours, which as you know is how long the classes I teach in the first year of your Law Degree last. You will remember that time you were distracted by your laptop, and when I asked you a question to make you react, you realized that it made no sense to come to class merely to waste time. It is in class, conversing with you (as for me teaching is dialogue) where you let me know what you think of yourself, and sometimes even what you feel about yourself. You could sum it up in a single paragraph.

You are young, but you have done everything. You have had particularly good times, but perhaps you have also suffered a lot, probably too much for your age. This has made you think that there are many circumstances that have not helped you. In some cases, you have not received the affection and security you wanted at home. In another case, the school environment made you suffer and did not contribute to strengthening your self-esteem. You are aware that the education you have received has not been the best: you have hardly been taught to read, to think for yourself, or to express your thoughts and ideas without fear of being wrong. You have had to learn that reality is complex and that not everything is black and white, and that to access it you must think, listen, and dialogue respectfully and calmly. Now you also realize that the social networks that you used to think were as important as the air you breathe have become toxic, addictive and impoverishing. You can't live without them, even though you know that they waste your time, stifle your creativity and sterilize your genuine life project. You know that they also make you feel bad about yourself because, even knowing that nobody shows themselves authentically, there are always people who seem happier than you. It is easy to fall into hateful comparisons that tarnish your own existence and significantly undermine your self-esteem. Perhaps you have not respected yourself and you have done things that you would have preferred not to do. This may have led you to despise yourself or some parts of you and has caused you to lose self-esteem and confidence in yourself. This then makes it difficult for you to relate to others, because your experience has resulted in you seeing other people as dangers or threats. You close yourself off and, more fundamentally, live in fear. You live in fear of making a mistake, looking bad, being rejected or being a disappointment to other people. In short, it is like you are living as if you are dead, because the subject that lives is another without a life of its own, not you. Let me now make some suggestions.

1. Be the writer and the main protagonist of your biography. Do not allow anyone to write it for you or to take over your role. You lose yourself when you victimize yourself, through trying to justify your behavior or hiding behind how you have been treated in life and your circumstances (for example, family, school, friends, social environment, and lack of opportunities). Even if you have been disadvantaged by these circumstances, a fulfilling life depends fundamentally on you. Do not let the shortcomings of others, of society, or of the education system hold you back or place a ceiling on your life. Focus on what depends on you. To do this, try to know yourself better, accept your lights and shadows and increase your self-esteem. You need to focus on the good things you have and try to develop them as best you can.

2. Reconcile with yourself. Do not despise or reject yourself for anything you have done, said, or thought. If you have made a mistake, acknowledge it, forgive yourself and make peace with yourself. I know this is not easy at times. But do not forget that you are not what you do. You are worth much more. You are not as bad as you think you are or as some people make you out to be. You can fix what you have done. If you do not forgive yourself and reconcile yourself with your past behavior, you will not be able to live in peace, your character will become thinner, your relationship with others will suffer, and you will be unable to forgive others. Not forgiving those who may have wronged you is harmful. Try to forgive without judging the person who has hurt you and do not allow resentment to nestle inside you. It is poisonous, toxic, and highly flammable. Reject it completely.

3. Have a project: embark on something big that is worthwhile, that excites you and gives you a purpose and a strong motivation that drives your life and makes it easier for you to move forward every day in that direction. This will help you to let go of the distractions of desires which immediately gratify, but are both fleeting and empty.

4. Think for yourself. Stop taking refuge in what others think, do and say. Take a real interest in knowing what *you* really think about things. Only then will you be able to do what *you* really want. When you are not the one who thinks, you do not do what you really want to do (no one likes to admit that their apparent freedom leaves much to be desired). Sometimes you are aware of this, but you prefer to continue acting this way for fear of being wrong. This is because it is easier to be wrong for having done what others had told you or expected of you, than to be wrong when it is you who decided what to do. This is especially so when your decision goes against the majority view. Do not stop thinking for yourself for fear of being wrong: it is better to be wrong having thought for yourself than to be in the right having uncritically assumed someone else's thought.

5. Learn to express what you think and to engage in dialogue in a respectful and calm way. Listen to everyone with interest and attention, especially those who think differently to you. Try to understand their way of seeing reality. Talk to everyone, but especially with those who disagree with you. Respect everyone. Value people for who they are, rather than for what they do or say. Do not give too much importance to those who value you fundamentally for what you do or say, and give even less to those who try to impose their ideas upon you.

6. Spend some time reading every day. Speak with thinkers and writers who have preceded you or who you may never meet. Spend some time each day quietly reading. It is comforting because it reconciles you with yourself and stimulates your thinking. Reading will help you to think more, to express yourself better, to be more creative, to know yourself a little better and to gain a greater understanding of the world you live in.

7. Write a little every day. You can talk without thinking, but you cannot write without thinking. Writing activates the capacity to reason. I have more than proved it. Try it yourself: start writing in your diary, and write down every day something you have done, some event or some personal reflection. In a few weeks, you will have significantly increased your ability to think for yourself.

8. Don't fool yourself or let yourself be fooled. Things that are valuable cost you. They require effort, time, and money. If someone tells you otherwise, they are deceiving you. If something does not cost you, this may just be because it is not worth doing. Think about it. If you think you are freer just because you have more choice, you are deluded. Social networks contain infinite possibilities, almost all of them carrying immediate gratification, but they do not free you or make you a better person. It is the opposite: they tie you down, degrade you, make you more vulnerable, undermine your self-esteem and sterilize your existence. They have made you realize that not everything you have "consented" to watch or consume has contributed positively to gaining freedom. If you have come to believe that consent is the only thing that gives meaning to your personal decisions and relationships, you have been deceived. Do not keep wasting your life like this. Consent only to what makes sense, is reasonable and in accordance with who you are and, above all, with who you want to become. Free yourself as soon as possible from that trap to be able to live with sense.

9. Live in the present. Focus on what you must do in each moment, putting all your senses and powers there and look at the intricate details without letting yourself be distracted by things that are not relevant or worrying about the result of what you do. You should do everything with peace and enjoyment, without worrying about an uncertain outcome or future. Be constant in what you propose, in your lesson plan and daily study, and the passage of time will play in your favor. Lose the fear of being wrong: making mistakes is not the thing that stops you from being better, but the lack of courage that prevents you from making good decisions in fear of not being up to the task. Each mistake recognized and rectified brings you closer to what you want to become.

10. There is no stronger motivation or driving force than love. It is true that the stimulus and the illusion that a good project usually generates (n. 3) can drive us forward, but there are deep motivations that are much more powerful. A minimum of self-esteem and love for others (and for God, for believers) can have a much greater force, because doing something for the good of others stimulates our creative capacity and develops our willingness to voluntarily sacrifice ourselves for something that really deserves it. A better teacher is usually the one who appreciates and seeks the good of his students; a better businessperson is the one who keeps the good of his workers, suppliers, and customers in mind.

I do not want you to put any of this advice into practice because it comes from me. No. Rather, I suggest that you think about them for yourself and try to imagine for a moment what your life would be like if you decided to make these principles your own and integrate them into your life. This should be done after critically analyzing these principles for yourself. If you make that decision and are consistent with it, I can tell you what will happen to you. You will trust yourself more, your self-esteem will improve, you will be more respected, you will be less dependent, you will care less about what others do, say or think, you will stop victimizing yourself for the shortcomings of your circumstances, and you will begin to excel academically. You will have more professional goals and you will perceive a fullness of life with less dependency on the virtual world and more on real faces to share, talk to and enjoy. Maybe I am wrong (I am also wrong, as much or more than you), but you know that I tell you what I think and that I am being honest with you. If you have any doubts, or if you try it out and find difficulties, or if you find that I am wrong, I would appreciate it if you would tell me frankly (@anicetomasferrer; aniceto.masferrer@uv.es). Do not forget that you are worth a lot. All the best, your former teacher.

TEACHING VOCATION

Discovering my teaching vocation three decades ago was one of the most beautiful and important experiences of my life. Those who feel this way never think they know it all, nor do they see themselves as better than their colleagues, because they know that the accomplishment of this task exceeds their own strength. I know the deficiencies of the university system, as well as the shortcomings of today's students. This is a consequence of an education that does not encourage a taste for reading and writing, nor does it teach students to think for themselves and to express themselves in public. Nor does it strengthen their memory, which is essential for arguing, reasoning, and relating diverse realities and ideas. Although the university teacher is not a psychologist, they should know their audience if they want to teach or discuss. Teaching and learning require a connection the teacher cannot teach if the student does not want to learn. My teaching experience has shown me that there are five fundamental keys to overcoming the student's current shortcomings.

The first key is *illusion and its contagion.* The current generation demonstrate a certain reluctance or weariness, perhaps because they have everything without any effort or because they have been able to enjoy many experiences from a very early age. However, they maintain the ability to be excited and easily distinguish between those teachers who teach with enthusiasm and those who do not, between those who teach their subjects with a certain coldness and those who do so with interest and even passion. The teacher who teaches with passion tends to infect a good part of his students, who then infect others. Those students are infected by the enthusiasm and passion of the teacher. This is not a theory, but a reality. It is a fact of experience.

The second is *the search for the meaning of reality and the desire to know.* There is nothing more difficult (albeit not impossible) than undertaking to study something without having awakened any interest in it or without having felt the need to know it. Ortega y Gasset stated that "to teach is not primarily and fundamentally to teach the need for a science and not to teach the science whose need is impossible to make the student feel". The student hates having to study problems and processes he does not understand, and which escape him completely. The teacher must start with the need for the subject itself and remain there until he has succeeded in conveying this meaning to his students, as well as the meaning of each particular lesson.

The third is *the close and humble attitude, together with the reinforcement of esteem and authority.* Students are often aware of their limited training. As a simplified summary, they know that their knowledge is very scarce and that their teacher knows everything. This mentality conditions the teacher-student relationship by making it appear as a distant one, which alienates those who need closeness to discuss. As a result, students tend to adopt a passive attitude and avoid intervening. They are embarrassed to say anything or give their opinion in front of someone who will be able to discover the extent of their ignorance. Exposing their ignorance humiliates them. It is an analogous humiliation to that felt by anyone who is physically naked in front of a stranger. No action is taken to protect their modesty and good name. The teacher must get out of this mistake by promoting dialogue between himself and his students, without pretending to hide the truth that he does in fact know more than the student. Overcoming this preventive, distant and passive attitude of the student is possible if the teacher adopts a double awareness:

i) he should be aware that he too, despite having studied a field of reality in depth, is not capable of embracing it in all its complexity, and that he could always know it better. This is an idea perfectly synthesized in the famous Socratic statement 'I only know that I know nothing', as well as in Benjamin Franklin's famous phrase: "He who prides himself on his knowledge is as if he were blind in the full light"; and

ii) he should be aware that many of the students he teaches will be, in the future, better professionals than him. In other words, the teacher should acknowledge the current reality of his students while seeing and admiring them for what they can become. He should be aware that the latter depends to a great extent on his teaching. Hence the poet Hesiod's accurate statement: "education helps a person to learn to be what he or she is capable of being [in the future]", and not only to learn what he or she is [in the present]. The good teacher, aware of the student's 'total autobiography' rather than just the 'partial reality' of who the student is in the present time, adopts a close and humble attitude that facilitates his relationship with students. He is thereby able to gain their esteem while at the same time reinforcing his authority.

The fourth key *is trust and an eagerness to reciprocate.* Trusting and believing in a person is a remarkable sign of sincere appreciation and esteem. It has rightly been said that "the teaching that leaves a mark is not from head-to-head, but from heart to heart" (Howard G. Hendricks). The passage of time cannot erase the people who believed in us from our memory. Students get this message perfectly: they immediately detect which teacher matters to them and which does not, which teacher believes that they can become good students and professionals, and which teacher does not expect much from them. They also understand perfectly well that a good teacher is demanding of both his students and himself, and that a teacher's lack of demand may be because he expects little from his students. The 'Pygmalion Effect' shows that when students perceive that their teacher trusts them, they perform better because they respond positively to his reactions: a closer emotional climate is created, more material is taught, there are more questions, and a dialogue is generated between the teacher and his students. The teacher who builds a relationship with his students by believing in them and demanding more from them usually motivates them, which results in an eagerness to learn that facilitates dialogue between teacher and students.

And the fifth key refers to *a teaching method that stimulates and promotes the desire to improve.* A teacher must use a good method of teaching that stimulates his students' desire to improve for there to be any point in him teaching them the meaning of his subject, infecting enthusiasm for it, and believing in his students. Each class session should be a challenge for the student. It should be an opportunity for improvement when working with the teacher, and an opportunity to reaffirm the personal dimension of the learning process.

A teacher touches heaven in the performance of his duties when he feels as much passion for what he teaches as sincere affection for those he teaches. In his *Dialogues*, Plato presents Socrates as seducer, beloved and lover. Thought advances under the impulse of Eros, without which it loses all its vitality (Byung-Chul Han). I find a good class much more gratifying than publishing a good article in a prestigious magazine, probably because every single human face is more beautiful and worthy of being loved than all the mysteries of this world and the entire universe.

SELECTION OF SIXTEEN RECOMMENDED READINGS

Alasdair MacIntyre, *After virtue*, University of Notre Dame Press, 3rd ed., 2007.

Albert Borgmann, *Technology and the Character of Contemporary Life: A Philosophical Inquiry*, University of Chicago Press, 1984.

Byung-Chul Han, *The Agony of Eros*, MIT Press, 2017.

Byung-Chul Han, *The Burnout Society*, Stanford University Press, 2015.

Carl Honoré, *In Praise of Slow*, Orion Publishing, 2004.

Emily E. Smith, *The Art of Cultivating a Meaningful Life*, Madrid: Urano, 2017.

Jacques Maritain, *The Person and the Common Good*, University of Notre Dame Press, 1966.

Jacques Philippe, *Interior Life*, Scepter Publishing, 2007.

Josef Pieper, *Leisure: The Basis of Culture*, Ignatius Press, 1998.

Josef Pieper, *The Four Cardinal Virtues*, University of Notre Dame Press, 1966.

Marián Rojas Estapé, *How to Make Good Things Happen: Know Your Brain, Enhance Your Life*, Countryman Press, 2021.

Matthew B. Crawford, *The World Beyond Your Head: On Becoming an Individual in an Age of Distraction*, Farrar, Straus and Giroux, 2015.

Pico Iyer, *The Art of Stillness: Adventures in Going Nowhere*, TED Books / Simon & Schuster, 2014.

Servais Pinckaers, *The Sources of Christian Ethics*, Catholic University of America Press, 1995.

Thomas Merton, *New Seeds of Contemplation*, New Directions, 1961

Zygmunt Bauman, *Liquid Modernity*, Polity Press, 2000.

www.ingramcontent.com/pod-product-compliance
Lightning Source LLC
Chambersburg PA
CBHW052150090426
42741CB00010B/2206